BLOOM WHERE YOU ARE PLANTED

JOYCE PROCTOR BEAMAN

Moore Publishing Company
Durham, North Carolina

Copyright 1975 by Moore Publishing Company, Durham, North Carolina. All rights reserved. Printed in the United States of America.

Library of Congress Catalog Card Number: 75-34645
ISBN 0-87716-060-0

Dedicated
to
Jesse and Pauline Proctor
(my parents)
The Reverend and Mrs. E.C. Morris
Laura Bynum Wade
Peggy Dildy Gay
and
Other Christian Friends
who kept saying,

"You ought to write
a religious book."

ACKNOWLEDGMENTS

My appreciation to:

Laura Bynum Wade, of Snow Hill, for typing this manuscript.

Patsy Batts Proctor, of Selma, who typed a second copy of these pages.

Peggy Dildy Gay, of Walstonburg, who assisted me in countless ways, in writing and promoting this book, as well as Broken Acres and All for the Love of Cassie.

Helen Clark Collins, of Greenville, who so graciously assisted in editing.

Faye Apple, of Durham, for her assistance in producing this book.

Pauline and Jesse Proctor, my parents, of Walstonburg, who helped me in so many, many ways during the writing of this book.

Bob Aiken, Jr., of Snow Hill, for photographs for the book jacket.

Over one hundred people who agreed to be included in this volume.

The many, listed and unlisted, who encouraged me as I compiled these chapters.

CONTENTS

You and Bloom Where You Are Planted, 1
Prelude to Blooming, 3
Personality and Character for Blooming, 10
Now or Never, 15
Poetry About Others, 19
Finding Oneself, 45
Beyond Stewardship to Sharing, 50
The Sleepless Hours, 57
The Cry — Please Help Me! I've Gone
   the Last Mile of the Way, 60
Human Touch, 64
The Cone of Ice Cream, 66
Volunteer Gifts, 68
Take Care of Each Other, 71
The Roses Now, 74
Paying Special Tributes, 76
"Miss Lyde", 80
The Loveliest Voice, 84
Blossoms From Braces, 86
Hands That Answer a Prayer, 90
Blooms for Special Days, 94
Love, 95
My Parents' Hands, 102
Blooming Unto the Young: Part I, 107
Blooming Unto the Young: Part II, 112
Youth Bloom at Christmas, 125
For Those Who Are Older Than We, 127
Blossoms From a Wheelchair, 133
Prayer, 137
Death, 141
Worshiping God Through Serving Others, 148
Bloom Where You are Transplanted, 157

BLOOM

WHERE YOU

ARE PLANTED

YOU
and
BLOOM WHERE
YOU ARE PLANTED

Bloom Where You Are Planted was almost entitled "Others," for that is what it is about. Also considered were the titles "You" and "Us." But it was finally determined that, if it were called "Bloom Where You Are Planted," its meaning would include all three of these titles.

One morning, in early summer, just before I began to compile this manuscript, my mother and I were sitting under a shelter at the old family farm where my parents still live. We were shucking early garden corn which we planned to put in the freezer. After a brief period of silence, Mama asked: "What did you say the name of your new book would be?" To tease her a bit, I replied, "Now, Mama, tell me, as best you remember, what you think I said it would be."

She hesitated a moment, chuckled, and then answered, "Something about 'blossoming where you are.'"

"That's exactly right, Mama," I laughed; "that's exactly right!" – because this book, though brief, is about 'blossoming where you are!'

Many of us have said perhaps, "If I were a different person, in a different place, living at a different time, I could do thus or so or become this or that." This may be true, but the greatest challenge and our best hope, for this moment, for this hour, for this day, is to consider "blooming where we're planted."

All the poems, essays and articles in this volume are by the author of this book unless otherwise stated. All the people mentioned are from North Carolina unless otherwise identified.

This volume is not professional or perfect, but you, the reader, may use any part of it — its style, content, or thoughts (which were written or created by its author) as you would a recipe or a dress pattern — if God leads you to believe that it will help you to bless or lift another life.

PRELUDE TO BLOOMING

Resolving to Bloom

The first prelude or prerequisite in blooming where we are planted is resolving to bloom — and then doing what we resolve. How many of us have made resolutions and plans, only to break them or forget them later?

But this matter of blooming is serious. It is, if you like, sacred. God commanded: "... Thou shalt love thy neighbor as thyself" (Leviticus 19:18). Jesus said: "A new commandment I give unto you, That ye love one another; as I have loved you, that ye also love one another" (John 13:34). "Let your light so shine..." (Matthew 5:16). "Inasmuch as ye have done it unto one of the least of these my brethren, ye have done it unto me" (Matthew 25:40).

So the first problem is resolving to do, which involves determination, willpower, and thinking. Proverbs 23:7 says, "As he (a man) thinketh in his heart, so is he." We are what we think — not what we think we are, but what we think. John Milton wrote: "The mind is its own place, and in itself can make a Heav'n of Hell, a Hell of Heav'n." So let's begin by thinking "others" — care, concern, love!

Consider these words which I penned several years ago:

Stretch forth thy hands
To the left, to the right;
Look now at thy body
It is, alas, a Cross!

Study thou your great symbol
For a moment, pause just now;
Wherever you go, you take it
Your body, the shape of the Cross!

Look thou at the creation
Humbly, look that way;
From Alpha to Omega
Your body, the symbol of the Cross!

Notice thou thy form
Think now, remember;
From His day to our day
Your body, the mark of the Cross!

Move thou gently forward
Carefully, prayerfully;
Remember thou art to thy brother
The sign of the Cross.

Finding the Time to Bloom

    The second prelude is finding the time. Our first thought is "How can I find the time?" The answer is simple: If this thing we call "blooming unto others" gets in "our blood and mind and heart," we will find time, and I might add, it will not be a burden, but will become the greatest joy we have ever found beyond Christ — and do you not agree that this is Christ, in action!

Henry Wadsworth Longfellow, many years ago, wrote a great truth:

> Heights of great men reached and kept,
> Were not attained by sudden flight,
> But they while their companions slept
> Were toiling upward in the night.

This venture has nothing to do with greatness, but the meaning of Longfellow's words to us might be that some things must often be done while the rest of the world sleeps. So we prepare our blooms in the early morning or late at night, while the rest of the world slumbers. Or we do it while we are standing at our dresser waiting for our hair to curl, or while we are sitting at the kitchen table waiting for the chicken to fry — in the case of writing a letter, or a poem, for example. We think it and plan it while we are plowing a field, or driving a truck, or waiting on a customer, or typing a letter, or riding in our car or on the bus to work.

The undebated truth is that we will find the time, and it will not be a burden.

Watching Our Motives in Blooming

The third prerequisite is watching our motives. To me, to do something in the name of the Lord for one's own self-praise or glory is blasphemy and desecration of all holy things. It is true that Jesus said, "Let your light so shine before men that they may see your good works and glorify your Father which is in heaven" (Matthew 5:16). Yet Paul writes in Ephesians 2:8-9: "For by grace are we saved through faith; and that not of yourselves: it is the gift of God: Not of works, let any man should boast. For we are His workmanship, created in Christ Jesus unto good works, which God hath before ordained that we should walk in them." So we are saved by grace through faith, and our works are the outgrowth of our love for Christ as His love burns within us unto others.

I have two beliefs, the truths of which I have not yet been able to deny: First, it does not matter, in God's kingdom, who does the job or who gets the credit — just so the job gets done. Second, I am convinced that what we get credit for on earth, we get little or no credit for in heaven.

The words of Jesus are sufficient here as He spoke them in Mark 12:38, 39, and 40: "And He said unto them in His doctrine, Beware of the scribes which love to go in long clothing and love salutations in the marketplace. And the chief seats in the synagogue, and the uppermost rooms at feasts: which devour widow's houses, and for a pretense make long prayers: these shall receive greater damnation."

And so, we must watch our motives. Yet, there is a strange, almost uncontrollable paradox about all this. Galatians 6:2 says: "Bear ye one another's burdens, and so fulfill the law of Christ." Romans 12:15-16 challenges us: "Rejoice with them that do rejoice, and weep with them that weep. Be of the same mind one toward another. . ." The paradox is obvious: As we fulfill the command of Christ, in loving and serving others, we, ourselves, receive the greater joy — and we must be careful lest we let this selfish joy motivate us. I am reminded of Helen Steiner Rice's thought that flowers always leave fragrance on the hands that bestow them. Maybe the answer lies in the secret things we do — and in a prayer that God will keep our motives pure.

Avoiding Vanity in Blooming

Fourth, we must be careful lest we become fanatical or overbearing about this venture. Basically, this is a quiet, personal, secret kind of thing. We simply tune our lives with God, with a prayer, and then listen to that "still small voice." (I Kings 19:12). He will, from time to time, call us or send us or speak to us His own way.

Fifth, there may be those who do not want our love, our attention, or our blossoms. The words of Karma, in the poem, "Anyway," may suffice here.

People are unreasonable, illogical and self
centered. Love them anyway!

If you do good, people will accuse you of
selfish and ulterior motives. Do good anyway!

What you spend years building may be destroyed
overnight. Build anyway!

People really need help but may attack you
if you help them. Help people anyway!

Give the world the best you have and you'll get kicked in the teeth. Give the world the best you've got anyway!

Dispelling Fear in Blooming
Too, if we are misunderstood, or perhaps criticized, the words of Theodore Roosevelt may be comforting to us:

> "It is not the critic who counts; nor the man who points out how the strong man stumbled or where the doer of deeds could have done them better. The credit belongs to the man who is actually in the arena; whose face is marred by dust and sweat and blood; who strives valiantly; who errs, and comes short again and again, because there is no effort without error and shortcoming; who does actually try to do the deed; who knows the great enthusiasm, the great devotion, and spends himself in a worthy cause; who, at worst, if he fails, at least fails while daring greatly.
> Far better it is to dare mighty things, to win glorious triumphs even though checkered by failure, than to rank with those poor spirits who neither enjoy nor suffer much because they live in the gray twilight that knows neither victory nor defeat."

Aesop wrote: "No act of kindness, no matter how small, was ever wasted."

L.J. Cardinal Suenens once said: "Happy are those who dream dreams and are ready to pay the price to make them come true."

And above all, let us remember the words of Jesus, "...And lo, I am with you alway, even unto the end of the world" (Matthew 28:20).

Blooming Regardless of Our Faith

This volume is based, to a great extent, on the teachings of the Holy Bible. However, regardless of one's faith, the ideas in this book are recommended for consideration in our world of human beings, among whom, day after day, we must "live and move and have our being" (Acts 17:28). The *Public Speaker's Library* expressed a challenge in these words:

> "If you would keep young and happy, be good; live a high moral life; practice the principles of brotherhood of men; send out good thoughts of all, and think evil of no man. This is in obedience to the great natural law; to live otherwise is to break this great Divine law. Other things being equal, it is the cleanest, purest minds that live long and are happy..."

Again, regardless of our religion or our faith, we still live in a world of people — thus the privilege of blooming where we are planted!

PERSONALITY AND CHARACTER FOR BLOOMING

How well I remember, as a young person, that I believed that an ideal, preferred personality consisted of the ability "to talk loud," "to laugh loud," and to make enough noise to attract attention. One day in high school as an outgrowth of a discussion in our English class, under the direction of our teacher, Mrs. Betsy Williams (now a resident of Raleigh), I realized that, to have a good personality, one must not necessarily practice or possess these traits or habits — that a beautiful personality often consists of quietness, gentleness, and not-so-much-talk at all.

In that same class, we also discussed the difference in personality and that all-important word, *character*. The word *character* reminds me of the following beautiful reading, one of my most beloved possessions, which my mother found and pasted on a torn-away, green cover of an old-fashioned composition book. During my childhood, I kept it nailed on the wall of my room. Later, as an adult, I kept it in *Leaves of Gold*, another of my favorite books.

Character
Character is the web of life woven in the loom of time. It is stretched on the hooks of

adversity, washed in the valley of tears, and whitened in the frosts of disappointment.

Nothing known among men, or belonging to man, is of equal value; nothing can replace it, nor can the gold of a world buy it. It is all that man can carry with him when leaving the world — the one thing that cannot be buried in the grave, and the one and only thing that time passes on to eternity.

Flames cannot devour it, floods cannot drown it, neither can the passing of years diminish its value. Standing next to the Ancient of Days, it waits to be weighed in the balances of eternity — destined either for destruction or immortality.

It has truly been said, "He who steals my purse steals trash; he who steals my character steals my all."

Author Unknown

As I have grown older, I have decided that personality is character, and character is personality. Proverbs 22:1 teaches us that "A good name is rather to be chosen than great riches, and loving favour rather than silver or gold."

The personalities and characters of my teachers have had a profound influence on my life. Dr. Florence Weaver, of East Carolina University, not only bloomed with personality, but blessed with her philosophy and character. The following words were written about her, and are reprinted here, by permission, from the October, 1970, issue of *North Carolina Education*.

"I sincerely believe that we teachers need to return to college as much for inspiration as for information — and more so. It is true that there is inspiration in new knowledge and ideas received and in old ideas reviewed and recalled. But there is a select inspiration which comes from that which is real and even more meaningful than information — that is, the inspiration of a good teacher.

Let us consider the often used, yet the truest, most meaningful words, to describe inspiration — dedication, patience, knowledge of subject, depth of thought, sincerity, love of subject, ability to stimulate thought, but most of all, love of people — care, concern.

I know such a teacher. I looked forward to her class. I caught myself speeding a bit on Tuesday nights and humming unconsciously on my way home. I happily went to class; I came away happier and more relaxed. I told everyone "close to me" about the joy of the class, my own students, most of all. On two consecutive Wednesdays, a French student of mine said, "We'll have a happy class today." Puzzled, (I had hoped that all my classes were at least a bit happy every day) I asked her just what she meant.

She replied, "We know *you'll* be happy today because you always are after Dr. Weaver's class." And I was. And I think I shall always be — a happier, better teacher, and a better person, because Dr. Florence Weaver was my teacher.

One night she ended her class by lowering her head, folding her hands across the podium, and closing her eyes as she often did when she said something especially meaningful to her — and therefore to us and for us. "People are important," she said. Then she paused and announced, "You may go home now!"

Care, concern, and courage in a college classroom. Informal enough to be informative; formal enough to be formative.

I looked at the class of thirty-three students, most of them classroom teachers. Quickly, I figured. If each teacher in this class teaches thirty students, somewhere, tomorrow, in the classrooms of North Carolina, there will be 990 people made happier because of the inspiration these teachers carry from this class to their own classrooms. Not 990, but 1,023 — because there were thirty-three of us.

Philippians 2:1-5 describes a beautiful character:

"If there be therefore any consolation in Christ, if any comfort of love, if any fellowship of the Spirit, if any bowels and mercies, Fulfil ye my joy, that ye be likeminded, having the same love, being of one accord, of one mind.

Let nothing be done through strife or vainglory; but in lowliness of mind let each esteem other better than themselves. Look not every man on his own things, but every man also on the things of others. Let this mind be in you, which was also in Christ Jesus:"

So does Galatians 5:22-23:

"But the fruit of the Spirit is love, joy, peace,

longsuffering, gentleness, goodness, faith. Meekness, temperance: against such there is no law."

NOW OR NEVER

To everything there is a season, and a time to every purpose under the heaven:

A time to be born, and a time to die; a time to plant, and a time to pluck up that which is planted;

A time to kill, and a time to heal; a time to break down, and a time to build up;

A time to weep, and a time to laugh; a time to mourn, and a time to dance;

A time to cast away stones, and a time to gather stones together; a time to embrace, and a time to refrain from embracing;

A time to get, and a time to lose; a time to keep, and a time to cast away;

A time to rend, and a time to sew; a time to keep silence, and a time to speak;

A time to love, and a time to hate; a time of war, and a time of peace.

Ecclesiastes 3:1-8

The following essay is reprinted, with special permission, from the November, 1968, issue of *Farm Journal*. In this article, I have described at least seven ways we can bloom where we are planted.

Moments for Forever

"Our lives are albums written through
With good or ill,
With false or true;
And as the blessed angels turn
The pages of our years,
God grant they read the good with smiles
And blot the ill with tears."

The lines above, from a poem by John Greenleaf Whittier, are in my scrapbook. I think about them often: albums of time, pages of our years, meaningful moments. For most of us women, life is filled with many things — ironing, cooking, washing, housekeeping, rearing the children, helping with the farm chores. Important things? Yes. But then there are outstanding interludes — occasional moments of beauty or realization ... We pause to savor such a moment, knowing that this particular interlude is unique; it will never come again.

We listen to the words of a wedding service we'll never forget: "Entreat me not to leave thee ... Whom God hath joined together, ..." and sharing that moment, we know that life offers supreme joy.

We look into the tiny, puckered face of a newborn, and we know that God plans a tomorrow. We say sincerely to a husband when he least expects it: "You are wonderful; I am proud of you." Sometimes the appreciation comes *from* the head of the house. Either way, a universal hunger is satisfied — the hunger in every human being to know that someone cares.

We pat a little leaguer on the back, and he grows taller before our lives. A friend achieves an honor, and we clip the newspaper account and send it to him; we rejoice in his triumph. Or perhaps we hear a compliment about someone we know, and we hurry to spread the good word to that person.

We pause in a church, in the quietness when no one knows we are there, and somehow life takes on a new meaning, a deeper significance, and a stronger purpose.

We attend a funeral and we sorrow with those who mourn, even though we know — we *know* — that life and time extend infinitely beyond this grievous moment.

Also in my scrapbook, to stimulate reflection: "We live in deeds, not years; in thoughts, not breaths; in feelings, not in figures on a dial..."

Somewhere between the sunrise and the sunset, we take time, or it takes us. Duties, responsibilities, work — such privileges are the essence of our days. Birth, growing, marriage, parenthood, death, joys and troubles shared with others, spontaneous prayer: these are our moments in time — moments to hold forever.

POETRY ABOUT OTHERS

Every human life is unique. We are told that no two persons have fingerprints alike.

Have you ever admired a person because of a certain trait or quality? Have you ever yearned to express your admiration and respect for, or to, that person? Why not consider doing so through a poem written in free verse?

I think that the idea of writing poetry about people must have come to me after I had received the following poem, written about me, by Mrs. Ann B. Keller, of Lucama. Though undeserved, its beauty and thought touched me deeply:

To Joyce

by Ann B. Keller

You write in gold,
Symbol of pure love —
Symbol of yourself.
No miser,
You share your words,
Your laughter, tears, and life.

Your smile beckons
Your golden words intrigue.
But bruised by life's buffeting
One may turn away.
There is not room for more pain.

Undemanding, you reach forth
With love
To mend the bruised spirit.
You write in gold
Symbol of pure love
You live the golden life.

    You can readily see why the joy that this poem gave to me inspired me to write poetry about others.

    The following poems serve several purposes: First, of course, as a tribute to those persons included. Each of them has blossomed in a special way. The second purpose is to serve as an example of finding at least one trait, or more, to praise. The third purpose is to provide a free verse form which each of you may use as a pattern to grow your own blossoms for others.

    You will notice that I used the same adjectives or nouns more than once throughout. It seemed unfair to rob someone of a trait just to avoid using the word again. I am especially attracted to the word *compassion*. I am very much impressed by that trait—and to say that someone has compassion, is, in my opinion, to pay one of the highest compliments.

    Again, you may use the poems, their style, their words, their thoughts, or any part, to bless others as you choose.

Peggy

More than two decades
  span the time
    that we played the organ
    and piano
      together—
        at our church.

Countless times,
  our voices blended in song.

    She, too, was a teacher
      of children.

We were not perfect
  or professional,
    but there was a spirit
      of heart and mind and thought,
      that moved between us.
        We were friends!

Emerson said:
  "A friend is a person
  with whom I can be sincere."

      Honest.
       Truthful.
        Trustworthy.
         Sincere.
          Concerned.
           Full of care.

>   Listener.
>   Thinker.
>   Speaker of courage
>   and hope.
>
> Can one find
>   in one human heart
>   these worlds?
>
>   She —
>   She is the fulfillment
>   of Emerson's dreams.

(Peggy Dildy Gay, Walstonburg)

Laura

Every seed
  Every bud
    Every flower
      Was sacred to her.

She saw God in everything.
  In His world
    In His children
      In His ways.

She had enough faith to move mountains —
  Deep
    Abiding
      Genuine faith.

Her nimble fingers typed
  whatever I asked.

Her home was a haven
  for many
    for me!

To be more like her . . .
  In faith
    In hope
      In love.

(Laura Bynum Wade, Snow Hill)

"Miss Gertrude"

There was always a candle
   in her window,
      when her seven children came home.

It never went out,
   by day or by night.

For the light was always there
   in her voice
     in her smile
       in her actions —
         in her love!

The flame burned brighter
   and was even warmer
     when the father
     of the seven
     became weaker
      and frail
        and finally flickered
         away.

She still had light
   for him
     for them
      for all of us.

The candle still burns
   as she moves among us.

When our light grows dim
   we hunger
      to light our candle
     anew,
    through the one
     she bears
       for her Master.

(Mrs. Gertrude Dildy, Walstonburg)

Kay

We often watch television personalities
  with awe and wonder.
We often think of them
  as someone special
    or unique
      out of our reach —
        and they are!

Yet, one that I got to know
  was Kay.
She was indeed
  an actress
    a performer
      the hostess
        for her very special show.

But she was a human being, too,
  warm
    gracious
      friendly
        compassionate
        genuine.

There was no acting
  no performing
    about her goodness.

She was brilliant
  beautiful
    beloved.

To see her
  was like seeing
    your own dream
      come true.

For she was,
  and is,
    many things
    that many of us
    long to be.

(Kay Currie, Washington)

Rex

His answer came
  in the form of a letter
    almost before mine to him
      could have possibly arrived,
    I thought.

"Yes, I'll be glad to
  type for you;
    I would be very much honored
      and proud and happy
        to help you. . ."

Somehow I knew
  this would be his answer.

I remember him as a student
  in my classroom —

    Always attentive,
      eager to learn
        to help
          to listen
            to do . . .

    Always concerned about
      sloth
        and indifference
          and carelessness
            and unconcern.

Always busy
 with learning,
  with good thoughts,
   with good deeds —
    Busy for God!

(Rex Best, Eden)

Frances

Though she was
   gentle
     quiet
       serene,
she could calm
   fears and frustrations
     of children
       and all of us.

She never raised her voice
   or talked too loud
     or moved too quickly.

But with her eyes
   and heart,
     she listened.

She was a teacher
   and a counselor
     of children.

All of us yearned
   to learn the secret
     of her peace.

She moved among us
   with compassion
     with dedication
       with concern.

She was a unique personality;
   most of all
     she had character.

(Frances Woodard, Black Creek)

Mr. Smith

"It remains to be seen
   what one man can do
     whose life is completely
      dedicated to God,"

  he used to say
     at the end of every sermon.

He was a good man —
   a minister.
But he would have been
   a good man
     in any sense.

The children
   at the Children's Home
     called him "Pa Smith."
      And his wife
        was called "Ma Smith."
     The children loved them so!

I read somewhere
   that we fulfill only about
    ten per cent
      of our potential.

Maybe the answer is
   in his challenge:

"It remains to be seen
   what one man can do
     who walks with God."

(Rev. Stephen Smith, Beulaville)

Peggy Grady

That great giant-of-a-man
    the Big Fisherman —
      Peter,
        wrote in his second book:

". . . Add to your faith virtue;
    and to your virtue knowledge;

      and to knowledge temperance;
      and to temperance patience;

      and to patience godliness;
      and to godliness, brotherly kindness;

      and to brotherly kindness,
      charity . . ."

One word alone does not suffice,
    nor the eight:
      faith, virtue
        knowledge, temperance
          patience, godliness
            brotherly kindness, charity . . .

But these are a beginning
    of the qualities
      of this
        angel of mercy.

(Peggy Grady Ellis, Tarboro)

Betsy

Compassion should have been
    her name.

For she bore the desire
    to help
        to lift
            to heal.

She'd say:
    "Let me do that for you!"
    and she'd do it.

No matter the strain
    the long hours
        the sacrifice
            the effort —
with the coming of morning
    she'd "have it done."

If one had a pain
    or a problem,
        she'd never forget to ask.

The main word in her vocabulary
    was *you*.

She thought it,
    she worked it,
        she lived it.

Compassion should have been
    her name.

(Betsy Bryant Allen, Greenville)

Audrey

Quiet.
  Simple.
    Humble.
      Lovely and good
        In a very special way.

Her spun-gold hair,
  her sincere eyes
    her soft voice —
      I guess angelic is the word
      I'm searching for!

And yet there was strength
  and fortitude
    in her character,
      in her faith,
        in her ways,
          in her work.

As my student assistant
  she worked many hours.
Every day, years after she
  has gone,
    I still find
      secret things she did.
  In those four years
    every minute that she was
      free from class,
    she'd come to my classroom
      to work,
        to help,
          to lighten my load.

Somewhere though,
  she blessed others —
    for she received
      the school's highest award.

That she could do so much
  was a miracle
    and a mystery.

She was indeed
  quiet
    simple
      lovely
        good
          and brilliant.

Most of all,
  she was
    living love.

(Audrey Price, Stantonsburg)

Debbie

Her young hands
  were reddened and chapped
    from scrubbing the library tables
      and the shelves
        and window sills.

"Just don't do that!" I'd beg.

"But I really want to, and I must," she'd say.

She was brilliant
  and she was beautiful.

But she'd bounce into
  the library
    with more enthusiasm
      and energy
        and eagerness
    and she'd do anything —
      no matter the sweat
      or strain
        or sacrifice.

Her brow was often wet
  her hair damp
    and tangled,
      her hands reddened
        and chapped . . .

But she was beautiful!
 Inside
  and out!

(Debbie Whitley, Stantonsburg)

"Miss Rowland"

Her four children
 hurried to the school bus.

Their hair,
 their eyes,
  their faces
   shone with happiness.

In their hands they carried
 not only books —
  and sweaters they didn't have time
   to put on,
 but also "beautiful" ham biscuits
  still steaming
   from the oven and pan.

She'd stand at the door
   in cap, or bonnet, or hat,
     and apron
       and long dress,
and watch and wave 'til
   they were out of sight.

Sometimes
   we'd go by her house at night
   and we'd see her through the window —
    reading.
      Sometimes alone,
        sometimes to her children.

She was God's answer
   to the thirty-first chapter
    of Proverbs.

(Mrs. Roland Galloway, Walstonburg)

Debbie Garris

It's all in getting
  to know a person!
    She was a student
      of mine,
    And I knew her
      as a friend.

She went away to college
  to become an honor student,
    Homecoming Queen,
      and many other good things.

Yet, I really didn't
  get to know her
    until that summer
      as a young college graduate
        she came to our school —
          Assigned eventually
            to assist me in the library.

I suppose the best way
  to say it is this:

    In every way
      she went
        beyond the call
          of duty.

She did not wait to be told.
Sometimes she did not ask.
Somehow she knew.
She was
sincere
sensible
smart.
She'll always make
a super friend
a super worker
a super person.

She blossomed where she was.
Surely, she'll wear another crown
someday
finally —
A crown given by the Master.

(Debbie Garris, Fountain)

Mrs. Wheeler

Beyond my mother's lap
and my father's prayer
she was the first one
to teach me about God.

I must have been young,
very young.

It was she
who first taught me
to sing,
"Jesus Loves Me."

She'd hold up a tiny card
with a picture on the front
and she'd tell us the story
of the picture.

Later,
when I was still too small
to see over the heads
of the first pew,
she'd stand me on
an old wooden-box-stool,
and let me tell the story
of the card.

She was my first Sunday School teacher;
She taught me about God!

(Mrs. Lillie Wheeler, Walstonburg)

(One very personal note: Mrs. Keller's mentioning my writing in gold is a literal truth, though the other words are much undeserved. Each book that I have autographed has been autographed in gold ink, and many notes and letters I write are written in gold. Often I say, "I write this in gold because that's what I think you are – pure gold." If you wish to write in gold, you can buy ball point pens, that write in gold for about thirty-nine cents each. Too, I'd like to mention here that my favorite quotation, besides Philippians 4:13, which I often write beneath my name, is "In all the days to come, all that thou wishest for thyself wish I for thee." I do not know who first spoke these words, but I always use them in autographing, and often on cards inserted in gifts. If these ideas appeal to you, please use them, too.)

FINDING ONESELF

"Finding Oneself" gives examples of thirteen unnamed persons who, though unaware of doing so at the time, bloomed unto others, and thus found fulfillment and meaning in their lives. See if you can find yourself among those in this article.

Fulfillment! To a woman, what is the meaning of this all-important term? Is it realized through becoming the First Lady of our country, or writing a best seller, or being named the Mother of the Year? Perhaps. Yet, it could be, for most of us, a less tangible thing, realized not at a moment as anything to be noted; but rather, the day-by-day contentment that comes from doing our daily duties well. Could it be that perhaps one day from these duties, there emerges that little something that makes us unique, causes us to be loved by others, and without our awareness of it, helps us to find ourselves?

A woman sold butter, cream, and milk to neighbors far and near. Among her many friends, she was known not only for her quality products but also for her graciousness and hospitality.

A woman lived in a modest home; yet, she had the most beautiful flowers in the neighborhood. Blossoms from her garden adorned the stage at the local commencement exercises, the bed table of a sick one, or the church altar on Sunday morning. In the fall, she shared seeds and bulbs with everyone who desired them.

A woman cared unselfishly and untiringly for many years for her sick husband. Friends who visited them went away inspired by her devotion and dedication.

A woman of very moderate means, who had lost her husband and son through tragedy, inspired those with whom she talked through her faith and courage. If I had to write the name of the best person I know, hers would head the list. Others, I believe, because of her good life, would ditto her name.

A woman felt that she had given so little to the world; yet, she reared five children, all of whom are now serving mankind in a very special way. To her community, she will always be the perpetual Mother of the Year.

A woman became well known for her tasty cakes. At church suppers and at club picnics, hers were always favorites. Many depended on her for that special cake for a wedding, a party, or holiday.

A woman who knew how to listen and to keep a secret, knew the secrets, the hopes, and the worries of so many. Free from jealousy and prejudice, she joyed in the success of others. Countless numbers who turned to her for advice and understanding will never forget her.

A woman, not glamorous as the world judges beauty, almost always carried a lacy handkerchief that sent forth the aroma of rose sachet. Immaculately well-groomed and pleasant, she was an inspiration to many young girls who expressed the desire to be more like her.

A woman prepared regular, well-balanced meals, did the family wash and housekeeping, and countless other tasks. A minister asked her husband to tell him the secret of his success. His reply was something like this: "My wife believes in me and is proud of me and tells me so. I can't let her down." The world could see her excellent housekeeping and model home-making; perhaps many never knew that through the joy of her husband's success, she had found her greatest happiness.

A woman who had sought contentment through education and public work was blessed finally with a son. Through this blessing, she found contentment that other things could not give.

A woman touched the shoulder of a young man and said, "I believe in you. I know you can do anything that you want to do." Years later, after becoming superintendent of his company, he returned to say to her: "I have worked hard, and I have been blessed with promotions and success. One of the things that helped me the most was the feeling that you were pulling for me and that you believed in me."

A woman taught a Sunday school class for thirty years. The host of friends who attended her funeral were saying in essence: Because of her, I know the Master better."

A woman who experienced the rare honor of seeing her son elected to the Presidency, heard her son tell a friend who asked the secret of his success: "My mother prays for me," was his answer.

Could the secret of these be found in the idea that they unconsciously lost themselves in something greater than they were — and in losing themselves, they have, perhaps, without realizing it, fulfilled themselves?

Fame is short-lived and one's glory travels only a short distance from his home and neighbors. It may be like the hero who was being honored in New York. A friend commented that the hero must feel flattered that so many were shouting and cheering for him. The honored one replied: "Today they honor me, 'tis true, but tomorrow it will be someone else."

So it could be the little intangible things — things we never realize or take for granted. Our lives reach forth to touch others in countless ways that we are not conscious of, but therein, we find ourselves with an indescribable peace and contentment. It must have something to do with what the Master was saying when He said, "...Inasmuch as ye have done it unto one of the least of these...ye have done it unto me" (Matthew 25:40). Could it be that in so doing, we also find ourselves?

BEYOND STEWARDSHIP TO SHARING

Recently, I attended the twenty-fifth wedding anniversary celebration of Mr. and Mrs. R.E. McCullen, of Mount Olive. Following the greetings and refreshments, I was talking to one of their neighbors about the compassion and generosity of Julia and R.E. toward their neighbors and many friends everywhere.

"Yes," she said. "A few months ago, I lost my husband. As soon as I realized that he was dead, I breathed a prayer, as all of us would, and I cried, 'O my God, what am I going to do?' There was no one in the house but me, and suddenly I felt empty, alone, and afraid. Then I thought, 'Julia will come. Somehow she'll find out, and she will come.' And she did. Almost before I realized what I was thinking, she was there."

This was typical of Julia, and R.E., too. They first "bring themselves"; then they return home to prepare hams, pies, cakes, and other foods to take to the bereaved family.

Bloom where you're planted! To be the first to go and share and care when tragedy or death comes. What greater gift?

Julia shared herself and also the things with which

God had blessed her. She was a good steward. She harvested, preserved, and conserved until her freezer and pantry were full; then in time of need, she gave; she shared.

To be a good steward of one's blessings and of one's talents is good. To share gifts of the hands and hearts with others willingly and lovingly is beautiful.

> Betty Hill Bynum, of Snow Hill, bakes delicious, 'specially-decorated cakes of all kinds. She *gives them away* to her friends on special occasions. She baked a large, beautiful birthday cake for me. When my two novels were released, she baked what I call a "Cassie Cake" and a "Broken Acres Cake." I froze these, and on special occasions at my parents' home, I took them — and many enjoyed her "blossoms."
>
> Roberta Rouse, of Walstonburg, grows roses. She prepared arrangements for neighbors and friends — by request or "by surprise."
>
> Lillie Moore Baker, of Fountain, has given enough food and clothing and vegetables to the young and old, black and white, to fill this book, if all were recorded. Especially in time of sickness, the birth of a new baby, or death, if she visited a home where there was a need, if she did not have what was needed already at her home, she would go quickly to the nearest town and buy it to take to the family.
>
> Thelma Yelverton, also of Fountain, does all kinds of ceramics and art work. She decorates not only cakes and caters parties, but she also decorates, with painted designs, wedding invitations and other similar items — and gives them for gifts. Her talent and touch are always special; her mark of uniqueness and superior quality add many-a-blossom to many lives. Wiley, her son, created the ceramic praying hands which are now on my den shelf.

June Lucas, Mary Ann Whitley, and Debbie Garris, of Saratoga Central, award-winning, teenage typists, willingly and joyously gave their time in typing countless pages for others and for me.

Dr. Huitt Mattox, of Wilson, inspires peace and tranquility more through his manner than his medicine.

Alton Woodard, of Black Creek, drove a truck for Thurston Motor Lines, of Wilson, for thirty-one years, receiving his safe-driving pin for that number of years. He was a good steward of his own life as well as in watchfulness and concern for the lives and safety of others on the highway.

Helen Clark Collins, of Greenville, reached out to me as a young, frightened student teacher. She not only taught me "grammar with understanding," but also imparted to me all that she had learned. She was truly one of the most unselfish persons I have ever known. She was a good steward of knowledge and wisdom, which she shared so willingly with her heart.

Dr. Gloria Graham, of Wilson, inspires serenity through "a smile in her voice and eyes" as she cares for her patients.

Kippie Eagles, of Fountain, now 93, has been a perpetual blossom of Christian faith and love to all who have known her.

Ona Patterson Humphrey, of Mooresville, came to Wilson County in 1947 as Home Agent. Through her work she has inspired homemakers to grow in knowledge and skill and especially to reach out to others to share that which has been learned. Because of her influence, the yearning of home demonstration club members and others in our county is "You teach me and I'll teach another."

Anne Stanton, of Stantonsburg, inspired students and fellow teachers with the unique self-discipline and organization of her life as well as her work. In philosophy, in teaching, and in friendship, her life seemed free from "clutter" that would hinder progress and trust. Many students said, "I wish I were more like her."

Sally Batts Hall, age 84, of Stem, wrote to me constantly during the preparation of this manuscript, blessing me with her wisdom, courage, and philosophy.

Mary Liggon, of Wilson, prepared such lovely, unique floral arrangements that people at the church always said, "I know who arranged those flowers." My father has always said that anything done with loving hands has a special mark. I think her floral arrangements exemplified this philosophy.

Dr. Eugene Grace, of Moore Publishing Company, Durham, also reached out to me as a struggling young writer to accept my manuscripts, without criticism, condemnation, or rejection slips.

Mary Belle Hinnant, of Wilson, is a glowing Christian with depth of thought and depth of purpose. Her work with the youth of Wilson has added much to local appreciation of the beauty of the Arts. Yet, her volunteer work with the children at the Eastern North Carolina School for the Deaf, at Wilson, is truly beautiful. At performances involving children who hear and those who are deaf, the deaf perform so perfectly that one cannot tell the difference in those who hear and those who do not.

Dr. Walter S. Linville, of Wilson, has sought the most modern methods of painless dentistry. Because of his skill and gentleness, combined with his quiet manner, all anxiety involving fear and pain are removed.

John W. Floyd, principal of Saratoga Central High School, presented, in the spring of 1975, engraved plaques to faculty members who had performed special services in behalf of the school. For several, this was the first time in over fifteen or twenty years of work that those persons had received such a symbol that said "Thank you."

Peggy Mann, of WTVD-Durham, is as gracious and congenial in person as on television. She has that unique ability of making each person feel special and important. To be in her presence is to leave her feeling "a foot taller."

Annie Turnage, of Snow Hill, sixth grade teacher, teaches as much through the beauty of her classroom and her own personality-character as she teaches through her words of wisdom.

Earl C. Funderburk, superintendent of Wilson County Schools, blended, first of all, depth of thought and purity of purpose into his efforts to lead the schools of our county. Because of the influence of his philosophy, his own example of hard work, and his ideals, each of us yearned and determined to perform each task, great or small, even better.

Dr. W. Burkette Raper, of Mount Olive, became president of Mount Olive Junior College in 1954 with twenty-two students enrolled and a real estate value of $25,000. Although many have enhanced the growth of the college, and have contributed to its success, because of the personal sacrifice, brilliance, industriousness, and leadership of Dr. Burkette Raper (awarded an honorary doctorate in 1960 by Atlantic Christian College), Mount Olive College, in 1975, had an enrollment in excess of three hundred students and a campus valued at $3.5 million, with total assets of $4.3 million.

Mary Kathryn Albritton, of Snow Hill, has touched the lives of hundreds of children in Greene County through her beyond-the-call-of-duty reading-library program.

Joe and Geraldine Owens and children, Joey and Daphne, of Marshallberg, built their own home, shop, and recreation room with "their very own hands." Not only Joe's superior seafood cooking and Geraldine's tasty lemon pies, but also the hospitality and genuineness of the entire family make their home a haven of happiness for all who visit there.

Marie Ruffin, of Wilson, skilled seamtress for Burton's, sewed, mended, and renovated many items of clothing for me with "joy and gladness."

Dr. William B. Young, of Wilson, heals more with his compassion than with his prescriptions.

Elizabeth Hill, of Ayden, does so many wonderful things for others so quietly and willingly that we call her our "angel unaware."

Brenda Baker, of Charlotte, exemplifies Lord Byron's thought, "She walks in beauty." She and her husband, Roy, through their personal lives as well as through their work in cosmetology, have inspired countless numbers of people toward greater charm and self-confidence.

Dorothy Baskette, of Virginia Beach, has perfected the art of listening, a quality which she projects unconsciously to make one feel like the most important person in the world. Her loveliness and graciousness are enhanced by her deep, sincere interest in every word that is spoken to her.

Dr. Leo W. Jenkins, of Greenville, now Chancellor of East Carolina University, became president of that institution, then known as East Carolina College, in 1960. Not only has he put the plus in excellence in educational endeavors, but also in courage, character, dedication, and perseverance, he has constantly been that which would cause those who know him well to say, "Truly, this is a man!"

John F. Blair, publisher, of Winston-Salem, has preserved the culture of North Carolina through the many books of fiction and nonfiction which he has published over the past twenty years about our great state. Also, he has perpetuated his own ideal of excellence through the quality of both the contents and bindings of the books which he releases.

Do you not agree that we cannot live long enough to know all the ways to bloom, in action, in spirit, and in influence? Can we not learn from the examples of others?

And the next morning, the sleepless hours will seem like a dream — good dreams that you can make come true!

Do you wonder when I wrote "The Sleepless Hours"? You are right. It is the fulfilled dream of a sleepless hour.

THE CRY — PLEASE HELP ME: I'VE GONE THE LAST MILE OF THE WAY

It was a stormy night. Thunder, lightning, wind, and torrents of rain seemed to be competing with each other outside the hospital.

After I had finished my visits, I came downstairs to return my pass. A worker in the hospital saw me, came toward me, and said, "Joyce, I need help. Etta and Mrs. Holloman think you can help me. When can you talk to me?"

"My goodness! Thank you!" I said. "I am so sorry you are troubled. I don't know what I can do to help, but I'm willing to try."

"When?" she questioned.

"Now," I said. "The storm is bad and I can't leave now. Even if I could, I would stay to talk with you."

As soon as she had made arrangements to leave her work for a few minutes, she began to pour out her heart. "My husband died over a year ago, and I can't get over it. I have cried and prayed and read the Bible, and I still can't get straightened out. I've even lost faith in God and everything. I've gone the last mile of the way."

Her voice choked. Tears filled her eyes. She bowed her head.

I looked at her silently. I thought of Jesus on the Cross. I thought of Paul's thorn in the flesh. I thought of the times in my own life when I felt that I had gone the last mile of the way. I breathed a prayer.

Then she looked at me, pleadingly, longingly, with the cry in her eyes, "Please help me."

What does one say at times like this? Then I gave her the most truthful answer I knew: "I don't know what to tell you," I said. "But I'll tell you what I've told my Sunday School Class and other friends many times."

"Please do," she pleaded. "Tell me anything that you think will help me."

So I began. "First of all, we are physical beings, not spiritual. We live in a physical world, not a spiritual one. Because of this fact, sorrow, pain, death, defeat, depression come to all of us — suddenly, unexpectedly, undeserved. Someday we shall enter God's spiritual world, as your husband has done, where there is peace and perfect happiness, but until that time, we must struggle with the physical through faith, trying to understand."

"That brings me to the second point," I continued. She stared at me desperately. I felt so helpless, so unprepared for this. I breathed another prayer.

Then I continued: "As I've told my Sunday School Class many times, we must struggle to live so close to God that whatever happens in our life, we can feel that it is according to His will for us. To do this is not easy, but it is one of life's greatest challenges."

She looked at me and nodded affirmatively. "But," she said, "I have lived close to God and I've tried to understand, but the more I struggle, the farther away

God gets, it seems. How do you explain that?"

"Maybe there's a purpose in the extension; I don't know," I said. "Maybe God has a purpose in asking you to wait for the peace and understanding that you seek. Maybe it's like Job in the Bible. Maybe it's a long wait, but God comes in the end. Sometimes it takes faith beyond faith."

I stopped. I couldn't imagine what I would say next. There is a limit to our human understanding, to this physical being in this physical world. She seemed to understand that I had told her all I knew. Then she moved to a new question. "Tell me something else, if you can," she pleaded. "Sometimes, when I go home, I feel that my husband is there, in another room, and if I could go there, he would be waiting for me. Or if I'd call him, he'd answer." She paused to swallow the choke. Then she continued: "Even sometime when I'm here at work, I look up, and I can see him standing in front of me. Some of my friends think I'm crazy or mentally ill when I tell them this. What do you think?"

"What do I think? First, you are not mentally ill, not at all. What has happened to you is this: You have reached a depth of human love in your marriage that many people cannot understand. I am afraid that there are many who never reach this depth of meaning."

Then the thought came to me, and I added: "How do you explain the Holy Spirit of Christ among believers, and then deny the existence of the spirit of one you have loved and known in person so long?"

She looked at me, seemingly with relief and deep understanding, and said, "Thank you. Thank you so much."

We talked for a few more minutes. I could tell by the movement of people into and out of the hospital that the thunderstorm had subsided. Each of us stood, clasped hands, put our cheeks against each other, promised to pray for one another, and said our goodbyes.

As I walked out into the dampness and darkness of the night, my knees became weak and I felt faint. I was completely unprepared for the preceding experience. I sat down on the bench, wet with drops of rain. I wondered if I had said the right thing. I wondered if my words were acceptable in God's sight. I was troubled. Then I looked upward; the stars were out. Suddenly, peace came over me, for I understood that my words were not important and that they were not the real answer. My body was just the instrument or vessel through which God and His Son and His Spirit were communicating with her.

In a few days, I received a letter from her. "I'm better," she said. "God is answering our prayers."

HUMAN TOUCH

There are times when nothing exceeds the meaning of the human touch, actually reaching out to touch another human being. All of us have read accounts of children who were physically and emotionally affected because they were denied physical conduct with another human being. Children yearn to be loved, to be touched, and it seems natural for us to love children and to touch them.

Yet, all human beings, generally speaking, regardless of age, hunger to be touched, especially in time of sorrow or suffering. Also, it is very natural to reach out to touch someone that one has not seen for a long time.

Especially, though, we must consider the hunger of the old to be touched. So often, we visit the aging in hospitals, rest homes, or even in their own homes. We greet them with our voices and smiles, but if many of them could say what they really want most, they would say, "Please touch me." It does not have to be an extended, extensive, exaggerated thing — just a grasp and holding of the hand, a pat on the arm, or the placing of one cheek quickly and warmly against the other. It may involve putting one's arm or arms around the shoulder of another, or it may even be a quick kiss on the cheek. There's just something about the human touch that says, "I care." The next time you go to church or Sunday School, pick out the old and try to determine whether you think anyone has touched, within the last week, the old persons there. If not, if you can cultivate the ability to touch — meaningfully, sincerely, blessedly — then this may become your very special "bloom unto others."

Do you recall the story of the woman who had been hemorrhaging for twelve years? She said, "If I may but touch His garment, I shall be made whole . . ." (Matthew 9:20-22).

The reunion of the father and the son, in the parable of the lost son or prodigal son, is described in this way: "But when he was yet a great way off, his father saw him, and had compassion, and ran, and fell on his neck and kissed him" (Luke 15:20).

Mark 3:10 and Luke 6:19 record the hunger of the crowds to touch Jesus. The New Testament tells us that on many occasions Jesus touched those He healed. The word *touch*, or a form of it, is used over 125 times in the Holy Bible.

Do you believe you can transfer pain through the human touch? Grasp the hands of someone in pain. Hold them tightly and say a prayer. Do not doubt this until you have proved me wrong.

There is power and there is meaning in the human touch.

THE CONE OF ICE CREAM

Mrs. Evelyn Hayes Bass, who now lives in Wilmington, was a senior at Stantonsburg School the year I started teaching. She not only performed well as a student in my English class, but also served as class president. Active in many school groups, she worked very hard at school. Also, since her mother was deceased, she worked diligently and faithfully as mother of her family.

Evelyn told me this true story of her friend, Mrs. Ruby Hardison, of Grifton, who passed away on January 5, 1967.

At the time that Evelyn became acquainted with Mrs. Hardison, they were both working at the Grifton Clothing Company. Evelyn described Mrs. Hardison as ideal — as a mother of three children, as a wife, a friend, and Christian. Mrs. Hardison was a person who could never do enough for others, but would never agree for anyone to do anything for her. Evelyn recalled that in the days of her worst illness that Mrs. Hardison finally agreed for her to mop or vacuum her floors, or maybe even take some ironing home to do.

During the latter part of her illness, Mrs. Hardison received radium treatments which made her extremely weak and nauseated. Evelyn became concerned that her friend could eat almost nothing that did not make her very sick.

Evelyn went to see Mrs. Hardison every day at lunch on the days that she drove the car to work. One day she asked Mrs. Hardison if there was anything that she felt that she could eat. Mrs. Hardison expressed a desire for a cone of buttered pecan ice cream. Evelyn said that she immediately went to the drug store to get the ice cream, a joy which she repeated many times afterwards during her half-hour lunch hour — for Mrs. Hardison was able to eat the ice cream without becoming nauseated.

Before she passed away, Mrs. Hardison returned to her church for Sunday School one Sunday morning and asked for a few moments to give her testimony. Her subject was "The Cone of Ice Cream."

Evelyn related that she was not in the group when Mrs. Hardison spoke, but that, as she returned to that part of the church, several people met her with tears in their eyes. When Evelyn asked what was happening, several said something comparable to "You don't know? You'll see. Just go inside where Mrs. Hardison is." Evelyn said that she was so surprised, yet humbled, when she was told the subject of Mrs. Hardison's testimony.

Just a short while later, a floral arrangement, in the shape of a cone of buttered pecan ice cream, stood among the many flowers at Mrs. Ruby Hardison's funeral.

VOLUNTEER GIFTS

Have you ever received a "volunteer gift" — one that was not preluded with an invitation or announcement? Maybe these would more appropriately be called "love gifts." If so, you never forgot that gift, did you?

We are a society oriented to do certain things in certain ways, to respond with certain responses — thus the invitation-gift expectation.

But again, what about those "unsolicited gifts," the love gifts, if you like.

Michael Kita, principal of Kerr Lake School, presented me two pieces of art work after I visited the school near Henderson.

Delphia Shackleford, of Saratoga, called to say that I must have some of her iris bulbs and that she was sending some by "Mr. Paul."

Matilda Townsend, of Wilson, came to creative writing class with a big bouquet of roses "just for you," she said.

Sharon Shackleford, a student, "bouncy, bubbly, vivacious," knocked on my door one day with a vase of mixed summer flowers, "just because of *Broken Acres*' coming out," she said.

Dr. Leo Jenkins, president of East Carolina

University, Greenville, did a special painting of an old farm house similar to the one in *Broken Acres*, and even brought it to me one day while I was doing my routine duties in the library at Saratoga Central.

Mary Belle Hinnant, of Wilson, a member of my creative writing class, drove "fifteen miles, one way, all the way from Wilson," to bring me a floral arrangement for my "club meeting night." "I had the florist prepare these especially for you," she said.

Mrs. Ruth Hines, artist from Wilson, brought to class, and gave to me, a special sketch-painting of a tobacco-barn scene like the one in *Broken Acres*.

Rex Best III, of Eden, often sends especially-selected, beautiful cards "with a prayer."

Marianna Walston, of Saratoga, sent a floral oil painting.

Mary Woodard, of Black Creek, called to say that she had a bushel of tomatoes picked if I would stop by to get them after school, and that "the peas will be ready soon, and you can get all you want."

Hazel Little, of Saratoga, brought a box of divinity candy. "I made some for Mama and her friends last night; I made enough so that you could have some, too," she said.

Cathy Pipkin, of the Bible Bookstore, Wilson, offered to have an autographing party for me soon after the release of my first book. What a gift to a beginning writer!

Laura Bynum Wade, of Snow Hill, never failed to have a "specially-baked batch of old-fashioned cookies for me when I visited her.

I will be the first to agree that concrete, tangible gifts are not the most important thing — that a smile, a prayer, a thought, a handclasp are powerful and

precious. I recall the words of Peter in Acts 3:6: "Silver and gold have I none; but such as I have, give I to thee..."

Yet, sometimes a small gift can say what words cannot.

Have you ever received a volunteer, unsolicited, love gift? Moreover, have you ever given one?

Leigh Hunt, in the poem, "Abou Ben Adhem and the Angel" wrote:

> "... Abou spoke more low...and said,
> 'I pray thee then,
> Write me as one that loves his fellow men.'
> The angel wrote and vanish'd. The
>   next night
> It came again with a great wakening
>   light,
> and show'd the names whom love of
>   God had bless'd.
> And lo! Ben Adhem's name led all
>   the rest."

Do we truly love people? If so, do we find ways to show our love — with a thought, with a prayer, with a written word, with a smile or a pat on the back, or maybe with a volunteer gift of love!

TAKE CARE OF EACH OTHER

The telephone rang. It was Kathy. After I had said "hello," she said quickly, "It is lunch time. You're busy, and I'm busy, but I just couldn't wait another minute to call you to say that what you said to Ted and me (both assigned names) as we were leaving your yard the other day really made a difference."

I was puzzled. "What do you mean?" I questioned.

"You remember. You said to us as we were leaving, 'Take care of each other.' "

"As we were going down the road," she continued, "Ted said to me, 'Did you hear what she said?' After I told him that I had heard, Ted replied, 'I guess that *is* our first duty, and if we fail that, we've really failed.' "

Kathy explained that their conversation in using that thought had been the beginning of bringing their lives together again, in closer harmony and love. She paused, and then apologized for calling, wished me well, said "Thank you again," and hung up.

Before I write another word to explain this event, let me stop to say that it "scares me to death" to think of the power of our words to harm or to heal.

One morning just prior to the phone call, Kathy

and Ted, neighbors from a nearby farm, had stopped by for a few minutes. Ted was going to a small town nearby for farm supplies, and Kathy decided to stay with me.

As we had chatted a few minutes, Kathy said, "I don't have time to talk about it today. Ted will be back in a few minutes. But I don't know what to do. Ted and I are just about at our wit's end. I've got to talk to somebody. I love him so much, but we just can't seem to get along at all anymore."

She continued. Her voice and face were troubled.

I listened. When she had finished, I expressed surprise and concern.

"It's so hot," I said. "There are so many problems with labor and the tobacco and all. Maybe Ted's not himself. Things will get better."

"I don't know. I hope so. I love him so much. But I'll come to talk to you about it soon," she said, as one of her two children came into the room to ask for water.

She did not seem to want to talk about her problem extensively, so I respected her wishes. We talked of other things — gardening, housecleaning, church, and the weather, but I could tell she was troubled.

Soon her other child came in to announce that "Daddy has come back now, Mama," and she got up to leave. As we went outside, I reassured her of my concern. She promised again to call soon or to come back for a visit to talk.

The call did come as I recorded in the early part of this chapter. It was not what I had expected, but her words were what I had hoped for — that no matter how she said it, things were better between her and Ted.

It frightens me when I think of the power of words to heal and to hurt.

THE ROSES NOW

All of us have heard and spoken the age-old saying, "Give me the roses while I live." How often we wait until it is too late. Again, another way to say this is, "Let's bloom where we're planted — now, to the living!

Have you ever considered paying a special tribute to your pastor, your Sunday School teacher, a school teacher, or to someone who has shown special love toward you, your family, your church, or your community?

We had Senior Citizens' Day at our church with special services and a special chicken-stew lunch afterwards. But somehow, this did not completely satisfy us. We wanted to honor each one. So we set aside one special Sunday for each aged person or senior citizen. A brief summary of each one's life was read on his or her day. Then with the famous words of the television program, "Mr. Jay Smith, this is your day," we honored that person with a framed certificate entitled "Special Award," which was an award of appreciation. Later, we took a picture, in color, which we had enlarged and gave to the person honored.

Someone has said that a person's name is to him the most beautiful word in the English language.

Psychologists tell us, that for most people, there is a special feeling that comes from seeing one's name in print. Our Youth Choir director, Mrs. Peggy Gay, discerned this, so she printed and duplicated a small newspaper of three to six pages with special news about the young people in the choir. To these young people, that newspaper was roses — for their names, their work, their buds, their blossoms were in it.

On Sunday, July 14, 1974, several of my friends and I attended Appreciation Day for the Reverend and Mrs. Dewey Boling and their family at Calvary Free Will Baptist Church in Wilson. To set aside this very special day to commemorate his six-year ministry was not enough: that morning a love offering was taken to finance a trip for Mr. and Mrs. Boling to the Holy Land. Each person, young and old, arose from his seat and walked to a special box at the front of the church where he placed his love offering. Comparatively speaking, the congregation was small, but over five hundred dollars was raised to be added to other gifts given previously. It was a beautiful summer day. Outside, the sun was shining. Inside this little church, Christians were blooming and "blossoming" in God's love.

PAYING SPECIAL TRIBUTES

The following is a special tribute to the Reverend and Mrs. E.C. Morris and his wife. So often I have heard someone say, "I would do a special tribute to my pastor, my teacher or friend, but I really do not know how to begin." Neither do I! And who does? But you may use the one that follows as you wish — its style or format or contents — if it can help you to bloom unto others.

Tribute to a Beloved Pastor and Friend
The Rev. E.C. Morris and Mrs. Morris

Lives of great men all remind us
We can make our lives sublime:
And departing leave behind us
Footprints on the sands of time.

— Longfellow

The Bible definition of greatness is "He that would be greatest among you, let him be servant..."

Footprints...a servant...a scholar...a sublime life...a man of God...greatness...These words create only a beginning of thoughts of the Reverend E.C. Morris, minister for sixty years. Other phrases, no matter how expressed, fail to describe this man of God and for God:

Willing service without desire for fame, credit, or reward.
Thoroughness of work and pride in work —
care and concern — in every area resulting
in complete yieldedness to God.
Humbleness of spirit, kindhearted, gentle, patient,
understanding — yet firm in the faith.
Passion for knowledge and wisdom —
and a hunger to share that which is learned.
An indescribable love for people.
Faithfulness to his wife, loved ones, his congregation, his work, his God.

Thought, effort, and preparation preluded his many years of service as he received his ministerial training from Moody Bible Institute, Chicago, and Ayden F.W.B. Seminary, Ayden, N.C. Too, he holds a teacher's diploma from Evangelical Teacher Training Association.

His pastorates have reached to North Carolina, Texas, and Georgia. Several years in evangelistic services have taken him to all the Southeastern States and to the Midwestern states. For fourteen years, he served as Secretary of the Georgia State Convention of his faith, at which time he was foreign and national mission director. Also, he was secretary of the National Association for twelve years, as well as secretary of the National Board of Publications and Literature.

In his mission endeavors, he visited the mission fields of Cuba and India and made surveys for the mission cause in Lebanon and Palestine.

James writes that we are saved by grace through faith in the Lord Jesus Christ, not of works, lest any man should boast. Yet, through Mr. Morris' diary, kept daily, we find one of the most remarkable records of Christian service. The figures not only astonish us, but inspire us and challenge us as well:

Summary of 60 years of ministerial activities:
Number of times read the entire Bible 67
Sermons preached 8,683
Special messages 829
Funerals conducted 221
Members received 1,616
Baptized 653
Marriage Ceremonies 106
Number of Churches Served 44
Revivals Held 267
Miles Traveled 771,552
Received for Service $117,060.68
Given to the Cause of Christ $12,827.55
Traveling Expense $34,955.03

Whether we say that he is a servant who leaves footprints, builds bridges, loves people, cares deeply, or prepares carefully, one sees beneath it all a strength and a goodness flowing from a pure good life — a life that reaches outward to man and upward to God.

Any tribute to Mr. Morris would be incomplete without blending his life with that of his beloved wife. Genesis 2:24, Matthew 19:5, and Mark 10:7 tell us that a man shall leave his father and mother and cleave unto his wife, and they twain shall be one flesh. Ruth, of the Old Testament, in speaking of her mother-in-law, said on one occasion: "Entreat me not to leave thee, nor return from following after thee; for whither thou goest, I will go; and where thou lodgest, I will lodge, thy people shall be my people, and thy God, my God."

These passages from the Old Testament and the New have undergirded the love and faithfulness of these two servants of God — for they are as one, and whether it be a step or a mile they must go, they tread it together — in sickness and in pain; in health and in illness; in weakness or in strength; in working and in serving, they walk side by side — beautifully, willingly, and tirelessly to lead all those whom they meet to God.

When we thank God for them, we must always use the word blessing in the plural — not because there are two of them — but because their blessings to us are many, many!

"MISS LYDE"

This essay was written posthumously in memory of a neighbor of my childhood, Mrs. Jonathan (Lyde) Galloway. "Miss Lyde's daughters, Lorraine and Madeline, spoiled me, as did she. If you have a neighbor or loved one, do not wait too late, as I did. Write your love now!

A Moment for Eternity

Sunday, May 29, 1966

I closed the door to the funeral chapel quietly behind me. Many friends were there. A handclasp, a grasp around the shoulder, a tear, an unspoken word of sadness. Time, thoughts, memories. And then, almost suddenly as late evening came, all the people were gone — all of them, and only I was left. I stood there before one I had known and loved for many years — one almost three times as old as I. I stood there with all my grief for the moment and my regrets for the past — sorrow for all the times I had not been to see her or called her or written her a note.

So often, we become so involved in life that we seem to lose real life and its true meaning altogether. We fail to take time — and so time takes us. Then one day we find that time has passed and life has slipped away and we are lost in a vast emptiness of time filled with "things" and we have neglected what counts most.

But this moment was a miracle. With all the friends gone, God gave her to me for a moment, and through the silence of remembering, we had one last chance to be together.

. . . I remember the first pretty dress I ever had; she helped to make it. It was pink eyelet. The first time I wore it, she and her family and I went to church together.

. . . I remember how immaculate she kept her home. Even now, when I have done my best, I must say, "But it still isn't so clean as hers."

. . . I remember how willingly she listened, sometimes for hours, it seemed, to my childhood problems. I know she carried many of my secrets and the unknown yearnings of my heart with her, without sharing them with anyone.

. . . I remember how she used to encourage me to play the piano. She listened to my poor attempts and praised them as if they were perfection. She especially loved the hymn, "God Will Take Care of You." This, too, became a song of my faith.

. . . I remember how she always had time for me when Mama sent me to take milk and butter which they bought from us. We would sit on the back porch and talk for a long time — even 'til the sun was high. Then we would have to wait for the shade trees to cast their shadows across the road. Then she would stand and watch until I was safely around the bend of the road.

. . . I remember how her daughters would come to my house and say, "Mama told us to come to get you to spend the night." This was the greatest thrill of my childhood days. I knew this meant pull candy and cookies and everything good to eat; but most of all, it meant sitting on the front porch and just talking and talking. Then to fall asleep between the best smelling sheets in the whole world!

. . . I remember the corsages she helped to make for my music recitals. Even now, when I smell a rose, I think of her.

. . . I remember that she said she thought I was pretty; it was because I was young. It was she who was really beautiful. Anyone can be attractive when she is young and has every opportunity. Often it is only after we are older and our faces are marked with lines of patience and love and understanding that we have that glow that counts.

. . . I remember her quiet faith and the inspiration of her good life. I remember how happy she always seemed — how pleasant she was.

Today, for a few moments, I walked with God because I walked with her and she was with Him. As I walked there — or at times stood still or sat quietly — waiting between the coming and going of friends, the Master gave her back to me, and she and I talked again, though silently this time, through memory. It may be that we shall talk again someday. In fact, I know we will — if I can be a little like she was and all she wanted me to be and prayed for me to be. . .

THE LOVELIEST VOICE

No voice is lovelier than Mrs. Moses (Effie) Holloman's.

Over the years, I had visited many friends who were patients at Wilson Memorial Hospital, Wilson. Always when I was there, I was inspired and impressed by the beautiful, melodious, angelic voice of the person who spoke over the intercom. In a low, calm, confident voice, she made the simple routine requests such as "Dr. William Young. Dr. William Young. Report to third floor, please." Or "Dr. Mattox. Dr. Huitt Mattox, answer line one, please."

But, because of the tone of her voice and her manner of speaking, she spoke far more than the routine announcements and calls. Her serene voice seemed to say, "All is well in this hospital. All is under perfect control. Relax and rest in peace."

One night during the spring of 1974, as I was leaving the hospital, I spoke briefly with Mrs. Etta Woodard, a receptionist, whose husband, J.E., was a senior in the first class I ever taught. Etta was a lovely person — so congenial, so sincere. As I turned to leave, she said something like, "Keep in touch, and let me know if I can ever help you in any way."

I responded immediately to her offer. "You can," I

said. "Sometime when you're not too busy, I want you to make arrangements for me to meet that person with the lovely intercom voice."

"My goodness," she chuckled. "We can do that right now."

She got up immediately and went to the left end of the long narrow room.

"Come, Mrs. Holloman," she said, "There's someone here who wants to meet you."

She was a tiny woman with graying hair, keen blue eyes, and expressive hands.

Etta introduced us to each other. Then I said, "I just wanted to tell you that you have the most angelic voice I've ever heard."

Tears welled in her eyes. She looked at me for a few seconds and then said, "My goodness! No one ever told me that before!"

And from that moment, a very deep, meaningful friendship began. Her life is as lovely as her voice. Through phone calls, letters, and chats at the hospital, we kept in touch and became better acquainted. I autographed, in gold, a copy of one of my books and in the inscription, I mentioned her angelic voice.

A few days after she retired (that same spring that I met her), she called to ask me to pray for her granddaughter who was ill in Texas. When she made that request, without knowing it, she paid me the highest compliment — for no human thought is nobler than to express to a person the faith that someone believes your heart can reach the mind and heart of God.

So, through one hurried compliment at the hospital, I received the far greater blessing — in many ways.

BLOSSOMS FROM BRACES

The Reverend Ralph Virgil Whitehurst could easily qualify as the first name to be added to the late John F. Kennedy's book, *Profiles in Courage*, if Kennedy's book were revised. In the late 1940's, Mr. Whitehurst, now minister of the Christian Church, Walstonburg, suffered a crippling injury in a paratroopers' jump at Fort Bragg, N.C. As a result of the jump, his spine was jammed, eventually causing complete paralysis "from his heart down."

When he realized that he would be permanently paralyzed, he suffered all the agony of human defeat, frustration, and helplessness. Even though he had lost a young son eleven months before and had begged God to reunite him and his son someday in heaven, he temporarily forgot the desperation of that prayer and thought of taking his life. During this struggle, he relates that the Holy Spirit spoke to him and reminded him that he must accept God's plan of Salvation before he could enter heaven to see his son again. "From that moment, I gave my all to God, and God led me from there," Mr. Whitehurst relates. "Becoming a minister was the last thing I wanted: it was against my will. But the Holy Spirit interceded and God took over my life," he says further.

Following his call to the ministry, he organized and successfully established "Emerald Isle Chapel by the Sea," at Emerald Isle, N.C. — an interdenominational church, founded, among other reasons, to give coastal visitors and vacationers a place to worship.

As is mentioned in one of the poem tributes in this book, the Reverend Stephen A. Smith, of Beulahville, N.C., often said to his congregation: "It remains to be seen what can be done through a life that is completely dedicated to God." The truth of this ideal is proved by Mr. Whitehurst's success during the first nine months of service at the Walstonburg Christian Church: the organization of an adult choir of eighteen faithful members; the organization of a youth choir of twenty-five dedicated, enthusiastic members who have "prepared and sung" on television, at rest homes, at funerals, and in churches throughout Eastern North Carolina; and especially the addition of seventeen members to the church roll.

When asked whether there was any discomfort related to his paralysis, Mr. Whitehurst finally confessed that he suffered constant spinal pain. "But when it gets unbearable, I reach one hand toward God and the other hand toward Dot, and the three of us climb the hill together." Someone has said, "Behind every successful man there is a good woman." No statement is a more appropriate, truer tribute to Dot Whitehurst, the wife who often reaches out her other hand to join the hand of God to make the circle complete whether they are climbing the hill of pain or walking through the meadows of joy.

Mr. Whitehurst has courageously sought self-reliance

and a useful, productive life. Today, day or night, he seems indefatigable and inexhaustible — so much so that one would never know, unless told, that he is in braces from his waist to his feet. Yet, he walks and moves normally, even though he seems a little "taller" than the average man — not because of his braces but because of the height of his faith.

Mr. Whitehurst reaffirms the character and strength of countless numbers of American servicemen who have blossomed from braces, braces which became power, not a prison. He symbolizes the struggle of countless Christians who wrestle with braces — whether they be of steel, of strain, of sorrow, or of the spirit.

John Milton wrote: "Who best can suffer, best can do." More than 160 references in the Bible relate to suffering. George Macdonald wrote:

"No words can express how much the world owes to sorrow. Most of the Psalms were born in the wilderness. Most of the Epistles were written in prison. The greatest thoughts of the greatest thinkers have all passed through fire. The greatest poets have learned in suffering what they taught in song. In bonds, John Bunyan lived the allegory that he afterwards indited, and we may thank the Bedford Jail for *Pilgrim's Progress.*

Henry Edward Manning expressed his feelings concerning suffering and adversity in this way:

"We never have more than we can bear. The present hour we are always able to endure. As our day, so is our strength. If the trials of many years were gathered into one, they would overwhelm us...God allows one and then another and then removes both...But all is so wisely measured to our strength that the bruised reed is never broken. We do not often enough look at our trials in this continuous and successive view. Each one is sent to teach us something, and altogether they have a lesson which is beyond the power of any to teach alone."

As we face and endure the braces of life, perhaps this thought from the pen of Frederick William Robertson affords comfort:

"As the tree is best fertilized by its own broken branches and fallen leaves, and grows out of its own decay, so men and nations are bettered and improved by trial, and refined out of broken hopes and blighted expectations."

HANDS THAT ANSWER A PRAYER

You are familiar with the story of the praying hands, I'm sure, but because of its beauty and inspiration, let us recall it together just now.

In the last half of the fifteenth century, two struggling young art students, Albrecht Durer and Franz Knigstein, worked together to try to earn enough money to continue their studies. Because their labor did not leave enough time to devote to their studies, they decided to draw lots to determine which one would continue to work to support them so that the other could complete his schooling. The winner in the drawing of the lots was to continue his studies. Durer won, and as was planned, he promised to return later to help finance the studies of his friend.

Durer went away to develop his talent and genius and became very successful. One day he returned to Knigstein to fulfill the promise, only to learn after observing Knigstein for a short while, that hard labor had bent and twisted Knigstein's fingers so that he could no longer use them effectively as a painter. When Durer, overwhelmed with sorrow, mentioned this to Knigstein, Durer saw that there was no bitterness in Knigstein's heart, only great joy in Durer's tremendous success.

Time passed. One day Durer went to the workshop of Knigstein. Since the large door was open, Durer walked in without knocking. Inside, he saw Knigstein kneeling in prayer, his gnarled hands entwined in spiritual supplication for Durer's continued success. Durer sketched his friend's hands and later created the masterpiece known as the "Praying Hands." Art galleries and collections all over the world now feature Durer's paintings, but the "Praying Hands" outshine all of them.

The "Praying Hands," among other accomplishments, are symbolical of love, compassion, personal sacrifice, and loyal friendship.

How many of us have known praying hands? How many of us have been praying hands?

I recall immediately my oldest brother's mother-in-law, Mrs. Dolly Hines, who continues to live with Dalton and his wife, Ruby, in Cary. While Dalton was working on his advanced degree at Virginia Polytechnic Institute, it was necessary for Ruby to work outside the home. With two young children, Pam and Andy, this seemed an almost-impossible reality. Yet, Mrs. Hines agreed to stay with them to do all she could, not only to assist in the housework and care for the children, but to encourage Dalton "to keep on keeping on."

After he graduated, I wrote her a letter and sent her a copy of the story of the praying hands. Also, later I was able to find a white granite, life-size engraving of the praying hands which I purchased and gave to her. They were symbolical of her love and sacrifice.

Also, while I was writing this book, my mother

called me one day to say that the peas in the garden were ready to pick. (She and Daddy had planted a garden for me beside theirs. They live about five miles from me.) "But," she continued, "I've already picked, shelled, and frozen several pints for you. I will bring them when I come." I was concerned and insisted that she should not have done it. She replied that she knew I was busy with the book and other things and did not have time to bother with the peas. Countless times throughout the years, I returned from school only to find vegetables or meats that she and Daddy had brought and put on the back porch or in the freezer.

Betsy Bryant Allen, now Mrs. Walker Lee Allen, Jr., of Greenville, was another perfect example of the praying hands. During the time that she was doing her student teaching with me at Saratoga Central, countless times she "grabbed" from my desk papers to grade, or lesson plans to copy, or accreditation units to type. Even now, to say that her hands offer twenty-four hour service for others would not be an exaggeration.

In July, 1974, I borrowed Daddy's electric hedge clippers. Mama cautioned me about the dangers of using them. Not long after I had returned home, the telephone rang and Mama said, "Your daddy is coming over in just a few minutes to help you clip your shrubs if you plan to be there."

No insisting that they not come, that I could clip the shrubs, would do. They came. Daddy clipped; Mama and I raked the debris. Another example of praying hands in action.

Bob Aiken, Jr., photographer, of Snow Hill, has made group pictures for over twenty years for the school yearbook which I have sponsored. He has never had to retake a single picture! Such skill and perfection do not just happen: they are the answer to a prayer!

In my Grandmother's bedroom there was a large picture of Christ kneeling in the Garden of Gethsemane, His hands folded in prayer, His eyes lifted toward heaven. Over the years I have seen many hands in prayer — and they are beautiful! I have also seen many other hands in prayer, but that prayer was a picture of labor and work and love for another's good.

BLOOMS FOR SPECIAL DAYS

We do not forget the special services of Christmas, Easter, and Thanksgiving. But how often do we plan, at our church or in clubs or other groups, special services or remembrances for such days as Mother's Day, Father's Day, and the Fourth of July?

Libraries have many books with readings or poetry or information about special days. I especially like Proverbs 31:10-31 and "Prayer for a Daughter," by George Webster Davis, for Mother's Day. Psalm I and "Prayer for a Son" by Douglas MacArthur are good for Father's Day. There are many beautiful readings on freedom and patriotism, and one can always sing "America," "The Star Spangled Banner," "God Bless America," and "America, the Beautiful." These songs are effective when read as poetry also.

Perhaps no one in your group has ever thought of doing something on these special days — another opportunity for you to grow, enjoy, and to bless.

LOVE

Human love, as it expresses itself through marriage, the home, the family, has inspired some of the most beautiful words from the pen of man.

Someone has said that "Charity begins at home," or paraphrased, "Blooming begins with the family." Proverbs 22:6 challenges us to "train up a child in the way he should go..."

Genesis 2:24 says: "Therefore shall a man leave his father and mother and shall cleave unto his wife: and they shall be one flesh."

Let us consider these poems as they project the love of the human heart for another.

        God is always with us.

        But there are times
            when He is very near.

            When a child is born.
            When a life returns to Him.
            When a soul comes to Him.
            When a prayer is breathed.

But when our lives
   our minds
     our bodies
       and souls

are blended in the love
  with which He sealed us,
    there is no time
      or space
        or breadth
          or depth
            or height

   only us —
    you and me!

And God is very near!

I do not know
   what I shall touch first
     when I see you.

I think I shall
   cup the palms of my hands
     around your ears
       and grasp the burning,
         almost swollen edges
           in my finger tips.

Or run the tips of my fingers
   against your lips
     or the lashes of your eyes.

Or feel the softness of your hair
   or the strength of your hands
     in mine — as I grasp them
       and stand away a bit
         still holding
           and look at you.

Or the touch of my chest against yours
   with hands moved up against
     the strength of your back and shoulders. . .
       as my face touches yours.

I hunger for your touch.

   I hunger. . .

      What shall I touch first?

I wish I could
   hear you resting at night.

The deep, heavy breathing
  the sudden jerk
    or grunted complaint
      when you relax —
    half-asleep.

Or the effortless snoring
  or the blowing of
    little puffs of air
      through your lips
       like a little boy —

    So I could reach out
      and touch your face
    So you would stop snoring
      and puffing. . .

    And fall into a quiet sleep

      so I would have to listen hard

      to be sure you were there.

      As I awaited the
      perfect rest
        of the morning. . .

The snows came

    softly
     silently
      unexpectedly

    in the night.

I had no warning
That they would be.

    When the warm winds of spring
      touch my face,
        I love you.

    When the crisp autumn
      nips my cheeks

    When the sudden breezes of summer
      cool my burning face,
        I love you.

But when the snows came,
all was numb.

    For I had dreamed,

      Always dreamed

        of being snowbound with you.

    But now

      I am snowbound away from you.

The summer sun
  singes
    scorches
      and sizzles
        the earth to purify.

The winter snows
  whirl
    whip
      and whiten
        the earth to beautify.

The soft, spring showers
  fall
    flow
      and filter
        the earth to solidify.

The sun, the snow, the showers...

  Must they be in our lives
    our links
      our love
        to purify?
          to beautify?
          to solidify?

        Why?

I do not know
　when I lost you.

It was so suddenly,
　so unexpectedly
　　like the snow —
　　　So long ago!

I do not know.

All I know is
　the dark
　　deep
　　　desolate
　　　　emptiness
　　　　　of the lost years.

I do not know
　when I found you.

It was so suddenly
　so unexpectedly
　　like the snow —
　　　Such a short time ago!

MY PARENTS' HANDS

Is it not true that we often fail to show gratitude to the ones dearest to us? If a friend or a stranger does us a favor or sends us a gift, we hasten to write a note, call, or express our appreciation in a special way. But what about gratitude expressed toward our own family?

Because the following article is very personal, until the closing moments in the preparation of this manuscript, I determined not to include it. But the thought burned within me, "How can I suggest to young people, and old, that they write letters or words or expressions of gratitude to their parents, brothers, sisters, or others who have touched their lives?"

The following, reprinted from the September, 1960, issue of *Progressive Farmer* is not intended so much as a tribute to my parents, as it is my way of saying to you, "Write that letter of gratitude; write it today."

Dear Mama and Daddy,

Many seasons have come and gone since that fall morning in 1948 when I left our simple farm home to take the first step toward fulfilling your dream for your four children. I, the oldest, was leaving for college. Now R.P., the youngest has just been graduated. Today your hair is whiter and your brows more wrinkled. But you can see the results of your sacrifices since Dalton, David, R.P., and I have college diplomas.

Through the years many people have asked me, "How can your mama and daddy do it? How can they take a small farm of 52 acres (of cleared land) and keep a child (and sometimes two at a time) in college continually for over twelve years?"

I could not and cannot answer their question. To me it is like a dream or a miracle. But I was the oldest and I observed you closely through the passing years. I have tried to figure out, in part, how you managed to keep us in school. To many, these ideas may be trite, sentimental, and unimportant, but to me they are real and true.

You had faith in your Creator, "the Giver of all good and perfect gifts." Your ambition to educate us was a sacred duty, a road too hard and too long to walk alone. You looked to Him; He heard your prayer and blessed you greatly.

So often from the little things that you had said, I knew that one of your greatest fears was that one of us might be influenced by something within the college walls which might cause us to stray from the "narrow path." We had our influences and our doubts, but you had brought us up in the way we should go, and each of us was determined that he should not depart from it.

You had faith in each other — faith in your day-by-day struggle with your hands and hearts, working together, to obtain that which could not be won alone. You believed in the beauty and dignity of hard work, and united as one, you learned the joy of honest toil.

You had faith in us, your children. No sacrifice was too much for you to make for the four of us if we were willing to work. This we knew and we were determined that we would never let you down or disappoint you.

You had faith in your soil. Your love, Daddy, for your few acres of land and its ability to produce and reproduce with proper care and management was, and still is, almost unbelievable.

Many years ago, while writing an essay on soil conservation, you remember that I asked you for an idea to include. Your reply was, "Give the best that you have to the soil with a prayer and the best will come from the soil to you." You believed in your land. You did not fail the land; the soil did not fail you.

Hidden away in an old cabinet, I found a paper that you had started to write secretly, "As I walked and worked in my fields today, I thought I heard the soil speak to me..." And I shall never forget the talk you made at prayer meeting on the sacredness of soil from the Creation — how God had made it all and given it to us to use and protect as Holy Ground.

You had faith in your fellow man — your neighbor, your farm leaders, and your country. You cherished the right to live peacefully and freely with others in our great land of opportunity. You knew that the privilege of working to achieve your goal was yours to grasp for the effort. I never heard you pray without praying for your fellow men, your community, and your country.

Yet the way has often been long and hard in spite of all this faith. But most of the time you were blessed with good health and courage to press on. However, there were wind and hail storms, crop failures, and sickness. When you, Daddy, were critically ill with pneumonia, something I heard you say about wanting to live to see Buddy (R.P.) graduate made me know that you were determined to live if the Great Physican was willing.

There were times, too, when both of you really needed and wanted things, little things like shoes or a new suit or dress — but you always put yourselves last so that we four children might be first. Even the dimes and quarters you sent in our letters were symbols of your constant giving.

I must also mention our "little piece" of timberland. So often the neighbors asked you why you didn't sell the timber while prices were high, and you would always make excuses. I knew the real reason that you would not sell. There were four of us to educate; you could always fall back on the timber if circumstances demanded it. You would sell the timber — not for a new car, a new suit, a new tractor, a new anything!

That was our savings account. Many nights I dreamed that it was burning; but we were blessed, and the pines continued "to lift their leafy arms to pray." There was always a red pig, a Whiteface calf, a bale of cotton, some soybeans, or wheat to sell when the bills came due. And the old, faded green tractor could always find some "custom work" to do when the bank account got low. Of course, our banker, Mr. Horton, always honored our family by honoring your credit when other sources were exhausted.

And now Buddy is graduating. He is the last of the four. But we know that your ambitions for us have not been completely fulfilled. For your prayer now is that we shall take our places in the world — not with fame, glory and prestige — but with honor, humility, and holiness. Both of you have struggled that we might realize the joys of an education. So now may the four of us with hearts overflowing with love, gratitude, and sincerity say this to you — "The greatest lessons that any of us have ever learned were learned at home with you through your teachings and example." And when we are old, we shall not depart from them.

Love,

Joyce

BLOOMING UNTO THE YOUNG: Part I

    Born this day
        Unto us
          a child.

To be borne

    To hills and valleys
    deserts or fertile fields
    shadows or sunshine
As we bear him.

Born this day
    Unto us —
      children. . .

        Young
          Energetic
            Ambitious
              Eager
                Yearning, begging

    That we should bear them well
        to that place they must be borne
            before that final birth.

Paul wrote to Timothy in I Timothy 4:12-14: "Let no man despise thy youth, but be thou an example of the believers, in word, in conversation, in charity, in spirit, in faith, in purity. Till I come, give attention to reading, exhortation, to doctrine. Neglect not the gift that is in thee..."

One of today's greatest challenges, to the young and to the old, is that of "blooming unto the young." It is trite to say that young people, as always, are faced with countless problems. They look not only to their peers but also to adults to help them, to love them, to understand them. Maybe this thought is expressed, to a degree, in these words that I wrote for a panel participation at Delta Kappa Gamma Meeting in Wilson in 1973:

Into our classrooms they come —
    Teenagers:

And we become
    Not only a teacher
    But a mother substitute
        a counselor
            an authority on drugs, family life, football,
                the job market...
                A social worker
                      A trainer for life's work...

We see anxieties, frustrations, uncertainties...

It is a new day
    a new way
        a new generation...

This calls for a new strength
   a new knowledge
     a new way...

Or maybe the word is not *new*
   But renewed...

     Renewed strength
       Renewed knowledge
         Renewed ways...

           Of reaching out
             And especially of reaching up.

Or maybe these words from Camus best express our challenge:

> Don't walk in front of me,
> I may not follow.
> Don't walk behind me,
> I may not lead.
> Walk beside me
> And just be my friend.

I recall the following experience, reprinted here from the *Wilson Daily Times*, April 2, 1960:

> As I entered the local A and P Store last Saturday afternoon, I heard three little Brownie Girl Scouts asking several ladies to purchase Girl Scout Cookies.

"Oh, I've already bought a box," one said.

"My daughter sells them, too," another replied.

"I'm on a diet," the third one added.

I appreciated the courteous, sincere rejections of the three ladies, but remembering how good the cookies were that my little Brownie Scout cousin used to sell, I decided to consider buying a box.

You should have seen the eyes of the three little Scouts when they realized that I was a prospective customer! How eagerly they showed me the four kinds — all three talking at the same time!

I selected a box and told them I needed some change and that I would buy them when my other grocery shopping was finished. I requested that they put that box aside for me.

What a disappointed, dejected look covered their once-eager faces. They looked as if they were thinking, "That's just an excuse; you won't come back."

As I shopped, I kept thinking about the little girls and the promise that I had made.

The courteous salesgirl packed my groceries. On my way out, I stopped at the Scout table to get my cookies.

Again, their eyes beamed with joy. "You did come back," they seemed to say.

I noticed that they had several large grocery bags filled with many boxes of cookies. When I asked for my box, one of the Brownies started emptying one of the large bags — one box at the time. At the "very" bottom, she had safely hidden the box of cookies that I had selected.

"We had only two boxes like you wanted; so I put yours at the bottom of the bag so we'd be sure we didn't sell it," one said quickly.

I paid her, took my cookies, and left.

On my way home, I kept thinking about the three little Brownies. Suppose I had not returned to buy their cookies?

They were so eager to keep their promise to me by saving that particular box. Yet, had I not returned, three little girls' faith in an adult might have been destroyed. They would have learned quickly and surely that sometimes an adult's word is not his honor. What a horrible thing for a child to learn!

But most of all, I would have missed one of life's greatest joys — a moment's glance at a happy gleam in a child's grateful eye.

I like the words of George Eliot (Mary Ann Evans) as she expressed them in her great novel, *Silas Marner*, at the end of Chapter XIV:

"In the old days there were angels who came and took men by the hand and led them away from the city of destruction. We see no white-winged angels now. But yet men are led away from threatening destruction; a hand is put into theirs which leads them forth gently toward a calm and bright land, so that they look no longer backward; and the hand may be a little child's."

BLOOMING UNTO THE YOUNG: Part II

I am not a writer by trade or occupation or profession: I write for the sheer joy when a thought burns within me that I must share. Young people are my trade, my profession, my occupation. For twenty-three years, with God as my co-pilot, I have tried to work with them in three high schools of North Carolina — Stantonsburg, Snow Hill, and Saratoga. Therefore, they get three chapters in *Blooming*.

A few years ago, Dr. David Webb, then Director of Instruction, of the Wilson County Schools, asked me to write a poem to be used at the beginning of the Wilson County teachers' handbook. The poem was as follows:

Reach out

   To the young
     who eagerly await
       the beckoning of your hand and mind.

   To those who wait at home
     who confidently confide
       the sacred task of teaching their young.

To those who lead
  who willingly entrust unto you
    the daily tasks which await each one.

To those who walk by your side
  who come with human hearts
    seeking understanding and common goals.

Reach out

  To your own life
    your heart and soul and being

  To find the best that you are
    so that you may fulfill your life

      To others — and unto thyself.

Reach upward

  To the Source of all strength
    That you may know the truth

  That all thy wisdom and work
    Shall find meaning and understanding.

Reach

  For brotherhood
    unity
      strength.

With love
   hope
     patience
      peace
        mercy
           understanding. . .

Reach — with a prayer.

Following the publication of my two novels for young people, *Broken Acres* and *All For the Love of Cassie*, I had the privilege of visiting schools to talk to young people about writing. Always, I anticipated what each group would be like and then I wrote a poem about each. Several are repeated below. The ideas are somewhat repetitious, for I wanted to say basically the same thing to each group. Perhaps you would like to write a similar poem for your young people.

There you were
  Young
  Eager
  Bright-eyed
  Bubbly.
You came in
  Excited
  Hesitant
  A little happy
    Because I was here
      And you could get out of class!

"Teach me to write,"
  You said.
I wish I could. But I can't.
I don't know how.
I just do it.
"I've got to tell you *something*," I said.
I know what I'll say —
  Just write. . .
  The same way you

      Live
       and
        Love
         and
          Learn
           and
            Laugh.

                Just do it!

To my first audience, the Seventh and Eighth Grades at Gardner's School, April 16, 1970.

You're young
  free
    happy
      energetic
        strong
          good.

You're lucky
  because you have a good school
    good teachers
      friends
        dedicated teachers
          devoted parents
            interesting books —
              And a chance to learn
                and grow
                  and succeed.

I love you
  for many reasons, but especially
    because you loved my little book —
      even before I knew you
        and learned to love you!

Live, love, learn, laugh
  as you build your dreams!

And learn to love good things —
  Wisdom
    Knowledge
    People
      The beauty of the Universe
        One another
          And especially, *God*!

Written especially for the young people at Vick Elementary School, National Library Week, April 19, 1972.

To be born into life
  Is a miracle.

    To breathe
      To feel
        To laugh
          To love
            To learn. . .
              All are a miracle.

To see sky
  and earth
    and ocean
      and trees

To feel the wind
  and rain
    and the touch
      of one you love. . .
        These are a miracle.

To be here with you
  To reach out to you
    To see the sparkle in your eyes
      To share the smile on your faces
        To have your spirit touch my spirit
          To anticipate the dreams, hopes, and prayers
            in your youthful lives. . .
          Each is a miracle.

To find a friend
  and love him
    and understand him
      and accept him
        and forgive him. . .
          This is a miracle.

To find God
  And to be born unto life everlasting. . .
    This is the greatest miracle of all.

Written especially for the young people at Pamlico Community School, November 4, 1971.

You're young
 free
  happy
   wonderful!

Learn to do good things
 Like reading
  singing
   laughing
    thinking
     listening.

Love people

 Love goodness

  Love light

   Love life

    Love God.

These are for now —

 And they are eternal.

Written especially for the young people of St. Therese's School, Wilson, N.C., October 29, 1971.

When I think of the close
of this day —
And *you*!
I see a miracle...

For your life has touched mine
A new creation has been created.

Our world —
of sharing
thinking
getting to know one another.

We have talked
We have wondered
We have dreamed.

As we have laughed
learned
listened
we learned to love one another.

Our lives touch
God joins our spirits
to make today everlasting...

And our new creation of friendship
becomes a miracle...
Not of ourselves alone
But together with God.

Written especially for the young people at Bath School, Bath, N.C., November 4, 1971.

To sing a good song
  To play a winning game
    To learn a new phrase
      To write a book
        To succeed —
          These are good
            and pleasant
              and honorable.

But
  to know truth
    to seek wisdom
      to have faith
        to love others
          to find God. . .
            These are
              pure
                perfect
                  eternal!

specially for all the young people of Vinson-Bynum School, Wi   .C., April 24, 1974.

Your school is good
  Because you are free —
   To pledge to the flag
   To sing "America"
    And to say "The Lord's Prayer."

Your school is good
  Because your teachers are
   Happy
    Pleasant
     Good
      Well-educated
       Neat
        And interested in you.

Your school is good
  Because your principal is
   Young
    Energetic
    Alert
     Smart
      Hardworking
       And concerned about you.

Your school is good
  Because it is kept
   Clean
    Fresh
     and
      Neat —
       And you are well-fed
        By those who work with you.

Your school is good
  Because you study
   and work
    and listen
     and learn —
      And do your part to make it that way.

Your school is good
  Because you keep it attractive
   By your bulletin boards
    Your neat playgrounds
     And your smiling faces.

Your school is good
  Because you are young
   and free
    and happy
     As you learn to
      live
       love
        and laugh together.

Your school is good
  Because you love it
   and enjoy it
    and keep it
     and make it that way.
      But most of all
       It is good because you are good!

Written as a tribute to the principal, David Webb, teachers, students, and personnel of Stantonsburg School, after an inspiring visit with them on Friday, April 17, 1970.

Think tall
Live tall
Smile tall.

Forgive
Forget
Find peace.

Seek
Study
Serve.

Learn to work
To wrestle with life
And to wait.

Love others
Love truth
Love God.

Written especially for the young people at Springfield School, Wilson County, November 15, 1973.

YOUTH BLOOM AT CHRISTMAS

Charles Dickens wrote: "I will honor Christmas in my heart and try to keep it all the year."

How do we honor Christmas and keep it? The answer is obvious — through love, service, devotion, kindness, forgiveness, sharing — or maybe through a memory.

The Youth Choir of a local church will relive Christmas, 1973, many times in years to come, through a memory — memories of the joys and excitement of preparing a float for the Wilson Jaycees' Christmas Parade.

In November, the members of the group began to lay careful plans. Most of all, they wanted, in their float, to emphasize the Biblical Christmas story. Using a manger scene, with cast, as well as wise men, shepherds, and angels, they blended their religious theme the legend of the little drummer boy. The music to the song, "The Little Drummer Boy," was played by way of controlled loud speakers, and the thought, "Such as I Have Bring I to Thee," repeated the theme on each side of the float.

In addition to the theme, the Youth Choir, and its director, Mrs. Peggy Gay, decided to honor their pastor, the Reverend E.C. Morris who was first runner-up in North Carolina for Minister of the Year of his denomination in 1973. A large sign on top of the gold-color Monte Carlo which pulled the float honored Mr. and Mrs. Morris who rode inside the car.

Pulling 5000 gold-colored napkins through wire to prepare a golden-float trim highlighted the activities. Only an occasional overpowering hunger or thirst interrupted the fifteen singing young workers.

The float was prepared in the shop-office facilities of Alvin Dildy, of Wilson, superintendent of the Sunday School.

Christmas is many things. For these fifteen young people. it is riding on a float, sharing their faith — and storing childhood memories of a Wilson Jaycees' Christmas parade.

FOR THOSE WHO ARE OLDER THAN WE

The English poet, Robert Browning, wrote many years ago:

> "Grow old along with me;
> The best is yet to be —
> The last of life for which
>   the first was made..."

Victor Hugo expressed his feelings concerning age in these words:

> "Winter is on my head, but eternal spring is on my heart. I breathe at this hour the fragrance of lilacs, the violets, and the roses, as at twenty years ago. The nearer I approach the end, the plainer I hear around me the immortal symphonies of the worlds which invite me."

Today, with the increase in life expectancy, we have a greater number of older citizens than ever before. How wonderful! What greater blessing could come to our young lives than knowing that we shall have our own parents, our grandparents, our neighbors and friends with us a few years longer than was once possible?

> "God loves the Aged.
> He gives them greater visions
>   than the young;
> He puts the words of wisdom
>   on their tongue;
> And keeps His presence over by
>   their side.
> From dawn to dusk and on
>   through eventide."
>
> Charles W.H. Bancroft

One of the great teachings of the Bible concerns our care of the aged. James 1:27 says, "Pure religion and undefiled before God is this: to visit the fatherless and widows in their affliction, and to keep himself unspotted from the world."

What a joy, what a blessing, what an opportunity — to visit the old, the so-called senior citizens. Visit them in their own home, in rest homes, in homes of relatives, in hospitals, in institutions — wherever they are! Take them for a ride. Take them out to dinner, or for a cone of ice cream, or to visit their church again, or to visit a friend — or a million other things you can do together! Phone them. Write to them. Pray for them. Love them. Touch them. Look at them. Listen to them. Remember them on their birthday, at

Christmas and on other special occasions. Promise to come again — and do it. Resolve — and find your way in this "hungry area" of the world.

Have you ever seen anyone starving to death? Probably not, in America. Yet, I challenge you to prove that thousands among us, young and old, are not starving to death for a little love, a little attention.

Take a youth group to a home for the aged — and sing, sing! Sing to them, sing with them. (Get permission first, of course.) Pack a picnic lunch, ask the name of a lonely person, and go to that person.

Just a few days ago, LaVohn Lewis, our local postmaster, said to me, naming an old, retired painter: "Please remember him when you're sending your cards. He comes to this post office every day, faithfully, to check his mail. He almost never receives anything."

Tommy Manning, brilliant young editor of *The Free Will Baptist* magazine, chose to write a series of weekly editorials to honor our senior citizens. (*Free Will Baptist*: October 30-November 6, 1974). He asked, initially, the all-important question: "How often have we traveled over bridges made possible by diligent labor and notable wisdom of the aged members of our society?" Among his many inspiring, in-depth thoughts, he chose to quote lines from the poem by Will Allen Dromgoode, which as you will recall, concerned the old man who built the bridge across the chasm over which he would perhaps never pass again. Said the old man in the poem, when he was chastised for building a bridge which would serve him no useful purpose after crossing the chasm: "There followeth after me today a youth whose feet must pass this way. This chasm that has been nought to me to that fair-haired youth may a pitfall be. He, too, must cross in the twilight dim. Good friend, I am building this bridge for him."

George Eliot wrote in *Silas Marner*, chapter twenty: "There's debts we can't pay like (we pay) money debts." Such is our debt to our senior citizens — those among us who are a bit older, temporarily, than we happen to be.

To me, this chapter would be incomplete without recalling the beautiful sentiment of "Somebody's Mother," by Mary Dow Brine. As you read it, from time to time, call it "Somebody's Father," also.

SOMEBODY'S MOTHER

The woman was old and ragged and gray,
And bent with the chill of the winter's day.
The street was wet with a recent snow
And the woman's feet were aged and slow.

She stood at the crossing and waited long
Alone, uncared for, amid the throng
Of human beings who passed her by,
Nor heeded the glance of her anxious eye.

Down the street, with laughter and shout,
Glad in the freedom of "school let out,"
Came the boys like a flock of sheep
Hailing the snow piled white and deep.

Past the woman so old and gray
Hastened the children on their way
Nor offered a helping hand to her —
So meek, so timid, afraid to stir,
Lest the carriage wheels or the horses' feet
Should crowd her down in the slippery street

At last came one of the merry troop,
The gayest laddie of all the group;
He paused beside her and whispered low,
"I'll help you across if you wish to go."

Her aged hand on his strong young arm
She placed, and so, without hurt or harm,
He guided the trembling feet along,
Proud that his own were firm and strong.

Then back again to his friends he went,
His young heart happy and well content.
"She's somebody's mother, boys, you know,
For all she's aged and poor and slow.

"And I hope some fellow will lend a hand
To help my mother, you understand,
If ever she's poor and old and gray,
When her own dear boy is far away."

And "somebody's mother" bowed low
    her head
In her home that night, and the prayer
    she said
Was, "God be kind to the noble boy,
Who is somebody's son, and pride and
    joy!"

BLOSSOMS FROM A WHEELCHAIR

Bettye Mae Webb, of Wilson, and until recently a resident of Saratoga, has inspired many. I checked a thesaurus to find synonyms for *inspired*, and yet words such as *bless, encourage*, and *lift*, did not suffice.

Born in 1939, Bettye was able to walk normally until the age of nine when she was strickened with muscular dystrophy. From that time and through the eighth grade, she walked by using crutches. By the time she reached the ninth grade, she was confined to a wheelchair. Because of this, she was not able to enroll in school until midterm, but after that time, in January, she never missed another day of school.

Prior to this time, her brother, Frank, and her mother, were faithful in helping her to go from place to place by crutches, and later, by wheelchair. After entering the ninth grade, her classmates, especially Douglas Gardner, Jay Pennell, Billy Taylor, John Amerson and Tony Crady blossomed where they were and carried her, throughout her high school years, in her wheelchair up and down three flights of steps daily. In May, 1957, Bettye graduated with high honors as salutatorian of her class. Her beauty and brilliance were, at all times, matched by her courage and faith. Friends say that she is one of the most optimistic persons they know — and I agree.

From her wheelchair, Bettye has bloomed more than anyone can record or imagine. Yet, for the inspiration and example to all of us, I should like to list briefly some of her achievements:

1. Writer of the local news of the *Wilson Daily Times* and columnist for the *Evening Telegram*.
2. Author of many poems, essays, and short stories, several of which have been published.
3. Member of the Beta Club and Future Homemakers.
4. Office assistant in high school.
5. Active member of the Saratoga Free Will Baptist Church.
6. Member of the church choir and several church organizations.
7. Assistant teacher of the Young Adult Sunday School Class.
8. Class President, Young Adult Sunday School Class.
9. Town Clerk of Saratoga.
10. Notary Public.
11. Church typist.
12. Heart Fund and March of Dimes Campaign.
13. Secretary for her brother-in-law and brother.
14. Secretary for the Bottle Gas and Appliance Company.
15. Avid sports fan.

One of the highlights of Bettye's life is serving as president and coordinator of the Search for Action

Club of Wilson County. Organized in 1971, this group is made up of those in wheelchairs, on walkers, and on crutches, as well as those with speech defects and problems concerning hearing and sight. Bettye keeps a scrapbook of the club's activities and prepares monthly an inspiring newsletter filled with philosophy and poetical inspirations.

If I were to try to describe the work and volunteer services of such local people as Mr. and Mrs. Onnie Cockrell, Mr. and Mrs. Julius Whitley, Mrs. Frank Webb, Mrs. Ellen Annett, Mrs. Lucile Hill, Mr. and Mrs. E.T. Lewis, and Miss Mary Betty Barnes who also work with this group, their deeds would fill a book. Again, these have bloomed, in this way, and in other ways, where they're planted.

In 1974 Bettye turned to politics, and through enthusiasm, phone calls, and writing hundreds of personal letters, she helped to elect Mr. Onnie Cockrell, of Wilson, a co-worker of mine in the Wilson County Schools, as County Commissioner. Also in 1974, she aided a couple from India, Mr. and Mrs. Shanahwas K. Shaikh, of the Bethel Christian Academy, to obtain citizenship rights. This couple, had they returned to India as Christians, would have faced many problems and perhaps death.

In May, 1973, Bettye was pushed twenty miles in her wheelchair to raise $319.00 for the Cerebral Palsy Walkathon, in Wilson. Also in the 1974 Cerebral Palsy Telethon in Raleigh, she demonstrated her club's specialized bowling equipment on television.

Her blooms are innumerable — and all of them from a wheelchair. Bettye's heart and mind are always open to those who call — by letter, telephone, or in person. Perhaps her philosophy can best be expressed in these words from her aspirations for 1974:

To live each day to its fullest and touch at least one life in a special, personal way every day that God gives.

To spend much time this summer making a genuine effort to help change negative attitudes (in some of our handicapped members as well as other friends, and in myself) to positive ones.

To be a genuine "God-mother" to my two beloved "God-children."

To offer my friendship to all who come to me or need a real friend, and go to them who cannot come to me!

PRAYER

Many times I have said to my adult Sunday School class: "As long as you can pray for another, your life is not lived in vain."

So often we say, "What can *I* do?" or "I can't really do anything." But we can! All of us can pray. Alfred Tennyson, the great English poet, wrote: "More things are wrought by prayer than this world dreams of..." James 5:16 says: "...The effectual fervent prayer of a righteous man availeth much."

This book began with a prayer: so shall it end. As I began to attempt to compile this volume, I wrote many to ask for their prayers. Among those were Mrs. Kippie Eagles, Fountain; Mr. and Mrs. James Hunt, Sr., Lucama; Mrs. Matilda Townsend, Wilson; Mrs. Horace Baskette, Virginia Beach; Mrs. Kathleen Owens, Walstonburg; Mrs. Nancy McClure, Wilson; Mrs. Sara Schult, of

Oklahoma; Mrs. Catherine Moore, of Stantonsburg; and many others already mentioned in this volume.

Prayer does make a difference as the following true account proves.

Sara-Lizer

During the Great Depression of the 1930's, many babies were born at home delivered by a midwife, and checked by a doctor who came later. I was no exception.

"Aunt Mary," as we respectfully called her, was the only help Mama had when I was born. Though her skin was a different color, we loved her as our own. As far back as I can remember, everyone knew that she was surely over a hundred years old — though she was not.

Aunt Mary had a daughter named Sara-Lizer — whom we loved, too, and who also merited the affection of all who knew her. Like Aunt Mary, her hair, too, was gray the first time I remember seeing her.

One day, a tobacco barn shelter fell on Sara-Lizer causing her to lose her leg. For the rest of her life, she walked with an ill-fitted wooden leg, working regularly, never complaining.

I kept in touch with the two of them, and after I became a teacher, I continued to visit them and to help them in any way I could — though I was young and struggling, too! Sara-Lizer insisted that she pay me or repay me; I insisted that she owed me nothing.

One day, though, after a joyous visit, she insisted

anew that she come to sweep my yard or clean my house or do something for me...."anything," she said.

In a sweeping moment, witout hesitation or premeditation, I said, "Sara, if you really want to do something for me, pray for me."

Tears came into her eyes and she nodded her head in the affirmative.

As I rode home, I suddenly felt a new strength in my life. In a few days, others noticed, too. A member of my Sunday School class said, "Joyce, what's happened to you? You're different; there's a new glow in your life." And there was!

Months passed. I continued to visit Aunt Mary and Sara. Our fellowship remained the same. The prayers were not mentioned after I had told her on the first visit afterwards of the renewed strength they had given.

Aunt Mary passed away. I placed a red rose corsage on her shoulder and they buried it with her. Sara said it was the prettiest thing she had ever seen and she knew that Aunt Mary would be proud.

Years passed. Sara's hair became whiter. I knew that the strain of wrestling with life with one leg was taking its toll. I was ashamed when, at times, I realized, or feared, that I had become selfish in my thinking. "When she is gone, who will pray for me?" I often worried.

Then one night, the message came. I did not sleep that night. The next morning, I bought a corsage of red roses and placed it under her hand in the casket, for another friend had already put one on her shoulder.

My heart was filled with grief — and yet, somehow,

I did not feel the helplessness that I thought I would feel. I decided that my feelings must be numbed by shock and that the emptiness would surely come.

As I left the church, a young, tender voice called me. It was a young "follower" of Aunt Mary and Sara, whom I had seen at their home often.

"Miss Joyce," she said, "Miss Sara is gone — and I loved her so much."

She paused to wipe a tear.

"But I want to be like her — and I want to do for you what she did — her prayers for you. In fact, I've already started," she said.

I reached out and squeezed her hand. As our eyes met, words were not necessary, just as they had not been on that day when Sara-Lizer made her promise. Suddenly I knew why my strength had not failed — and has not failed me still!

DEATH

I used to be concerned when it rained on the day of a funeral. The rain seemed to make the day even sadder. Then one day a friend said to me, "Just think of it this way, even the heavens are weeping." I try to remember that thought, and it helps.

Death is a paradox. In our human reaction, we are deeply saddened; yet our spiritual faith rejoices that a soul has gone to be with God.

Suppose a loved one or a friend asked you to talk with him about death or heaven or eternity. What would you say? So often we think of "blooming where you're planted" in a pleasant, joyful way. But death is a reality, with all its pain and sorrow.

As I recall my childhood, I remember well, when facing the death of a loved one, or when talking of death, that my parents taught my brothers and me, with emphasis, that we should do all we can, in our human way, for others while they are living. Then, when death comes, our greatest tribute to the deceased is to try to live on — to perpetuate those things which the loved one believed and lived. Further, they taught us that although those who have passed away cannot come back to us, we can prepare to go to them.

The following thoughts are for your own comfort or for consideration as you reach out to touch and bless another who may question you about death.

LIFE THROUGH DEATH

John 12:24 says, "Verily, verily, I say unto you: Except a corn of wheat fall into the ground and die, it abideth alone; but if it die, it bringeth forth much fruit."

During the dark days of World War I, a young soldier, Alan Seegar, sat in the mud on the front-line trenches writing a poem that declared "I Have a Rendezvous with Death."

> I have a rendezvous with Death
> At some disputed barricade,
> When Spring comes back with rustling shade
> And apple blossoms fill the air —
> I have a rendezvous with Death
> When Spring comes back blue days and fair.

> It may be he shall take my hand
> And lead me into this dark land
> And close my eyes and quench my breath —
> It may be I shall pass him still.
> I have a rendezvous with Death
> On some scarred slope of battered hill,
> When Spring comes round again this year
> And the first meadow flowers appear.
>
> God knows 'twere better to be deep
> Pillowed in silk and scented down,
> Where love throbs out in blissful sleep,
> Pulse nigh to pulse and breath to breath,
> Where hushed awakenings are dear. . .
> But I've a rendezvous with Death
> At midnight in some flaming town,
> When Spring trips north again this year,
> And I to my pledged word am true,
> I shall not fail that rendezvous.

On July 4, 1916, at the age of twenty-eight, Alan Seegar kept that rendezvous, and someday, all of us will, also.

Writing in his first letter, John says: 'Beloved, now are we the sons of God, and it doth not yet appear what we shall be. . ." (I John 3:2). Already, we belong to God in an intimate, significant way, as children belong to a father. Our heavenly Father is worthy of our deepest trust. Since we do not know all that we would like to know about the hereafter, we still have questions. But He is the Answerer, and one day we shall know all the answers.

Most of all, as Christians, our rendezvous must not

be thought of as a rendezvous with death; it should be thought of as a rendezvous with Eternity.

Someone will say that such a thought is wishful thinking. We wish with all our being for a chance to go on living beyond this life. If we have nothing to hold on to but a wish, then it may not happen. But we wish it because we have hold of God.

Further, there is much we would like to know about immortality which we do not know. However, we have an Authority on the subject. The most comforting thing to me about all that Jesus had to say about immortality is that He never argued about it. He took it for granted, was sure of it, because He was sure of God. Always, there was a strong note of certainty in what He said about it. At the crucifixion when one of the thieves on the Cross beside Him said, "Lord, remember me when Thou comest into Thy kingdom," (Luke 23:42), Jesus replied, "...Today, thou shalt be with me in Paradise" (Luke 23:43). Not the slightest hesitation or doubt showed in His reply.

Again, we find Jesus speaking as an authority on this subject when John records Him as saying: "...Because I live, ye shall live also" (John 14:19). "...Let not your heart be troubled...In my Father's house are many mansions: if it were not so, I would have told you. I go to prepare a place for you...that where I am there ye may be also" (John 14:1-3). No arguing. He said this is the way it would be, and ever since, people have been moving along the paths His words blazed. Our faith finds strong anchorage in the strong faith of His authority. Our rendezvous is not with death; it is with Eternity.

Often, people find it hard to believe in immortality

because they feel that they are dealing with something that becomes strangely new only after death. The hereafter is an invisible world. But some things in this world are invisible, too. Who has ever seen a thought, or love, or hate, or faith? Or who has seen the wind or all-important air?

Scientists tell us that the body goes through a complete cycle of change every seven years. Think of babyhood, childhood, teenage, young adult, and onward. We have already had five or six bodies, but we have remained very much alive. These "deaths" which came to our bodies have not destroyed us. There is something immortal about us. We just keep changing until we change for eternal life. In "Our Town," Thornton Wilder wrote: "There's something way down deep that's eternal about every human being," — and he was right.

"All I have seen," said Ralph Waldo Emerson, "teaches me to trust the Creator for all I have not seen." That is good logic and good sense. As Alfred Tennyson expressed: "We trust that somehow good will be the final goal of ill...That nothing walks with aimless feet, that not one life shall be destroyed, or cast us rubbish to the void, when God hath made the pile complete..." George Frederick Handel, the great musician, his health, fortune, and strength gone, wrote at a feverish pace, in twenty-four days, "The Messiah." When the King of England heard that part of it called "The Hallelujah Chorus," he stood to his feet. Audiences since that day have risen to the sound of Handel's "Hallelujah! The Lord God omnipotent reigneth!" Death does not have the last word. We have a rendezvous with Eternity and God.

When the saints of the Old Testament died, the Bible speaks of them as "being gathered unto their people." David, facing death, said, "Yea, though I walk through the valley of the shadow of death, I will fear no evil" (Psalm 23:4), and "I shall dwell in the house of the Lord forever" (Psalm 23:6).

In John 11:25-26, Christ said, "I am the resurrection and the life: he that believeth in me, though he were dead, yet shall he live: And whosoever liveth and believeth in me shall never die."

Paul wrote: For me to live is Christ and to die is gain" (Philippians 1:21). In Philippians 1:23-24, he said, "For I am in a strait betwixt two, having a desire to depart, and to be with Christ, which is far better: Nevertheless to abide in the flesh is more needful for you." He also explained death as a seed planted in the earth to sprout to become more beautiful and bountiful in eternity.

We not only have a soul; we are a soul. Heaven is the home of the soul. As Abraham saw it, heaven is a city with foundations whose builder and maker is God. It is the place our Lord has gone to prepare for those who love Him. "But as it is written, Eye hath not seen, nor ear heard, neither have entered into the heart of man, the things which God hath prepared for them that love Him" (I Corinthians 2:9).

To see Christ will be glorious fulfillment for the Christian for a lifetime of effort and eager anticipation. To have the veil torn from our spiritual eyes and to be able to see God whom we have tried to serve and worship will be satisfaction and fulfillment beyond one's imagination.

Life is continuous; it never stops; it is everlasting.

And it grows better and more significant for those who strive earnestly to know and to do the will of God. The transition from the mortal to the immortal, from the corruptible to the incorruptible, from time to eternity will be the greatest event of our lives up to that point. It will not be the end; it will be the opening of new vistas, new glories, new beauties, new opportunities, and something more wonderful and satisfying than our human minds can comprehend.

In His last days on earth, Jesus gave unto each of us a last will and testament. It is not a written, legal document as such, but the words: "Peace I leave with you, my peace I give unto you" (John 14:27). "...A little while and ye shall not see me...and again, a little while, and ye shall see me" (John 14:19-20). "Verily, I say unto you, That ye shall weep and lament...but your sorrow shall be turned into joy" (John 16:20). Isaiah wrote: "The grass withers, the flower fades, but the word of our God will stand forever" (Isaiah 40:8).

Eternal life does not begin with death. It can begin right now, with Christ, and death will become only one more bridge to Eternity.

WORSHIPING GOD THROUGH SERVING OTHERS
(A Summary Devotional)

As was stated in the opening chapters of this volume, blooming unto others is just another way of serving God and worshiping Him. Printed here is a "talk" that I gave on September 29, 1971, before the District Woman's Auxiliary Convention of our faith. These thoughts include and repeat many of the thoughts presented previously in this book. If you are asked to make a talk, or do a devotional, you have my permission to use the material in this chapter as you desire (as well as any other material in this volume, as was previously stated).

Matthew, writer of the Gospel which bears his name, records in Matthew 4:10 these words which he quotes in part from Deuteronomy: "Then saith Jesus unto him, Get thee hence, Satan: for it is written, Thou shalt worship the Lord thy God, and Him only shalt thou serve."

Worship is loving God with all our heart and soul and life — and doing something to prove to Him that we do.

Worship is a constant awareness of God — and living to show that we are constantly aware of Him.

Worship is the supreme dedication of the mind in thinking about God — and acting in a way that He may know and others may know that He is a part of our conscious and subconscious mind.

How often we think of religion as a science that we must explore or explain; or we think of God as a power that we must question or quiver about. We worry and puzzle our minds — and the minds of others — with questions of how to worship, when to worship, what part of one's life to give to God, the purpose of life, the religion that is best, or even if there is a religion, or at times, if there is a God.

The answers to these questions are always before us — so clearly and so simply that we sometimes pass over them in our search. For if we love God, we worship Him everyday of our lives.

We enter a church in the quietness of a morning or in the calmness of an eventide, when no one knows we are there; and we sit calmly in a pew, drop our head on the pew in front of us, and we rest and pray.

Or we kneel and drop our head in our hands and pray, "God be merciful to me a sinner," or "God forgive" or "Thank you, Lord."

Someone once asked Calvin Coolidge whether he thought man could worship God in the open field as well as in a church. Coolidge answered: "You can, but you won't."

So we worship God in His temple by making a

conscious effort to be there — alone, or among others who worship with us.

A second way we worship is through the study of His Word. Paul wrote in Romans 10:17: "So then faith cometh by hearing, and hearing by the Word of God." The psalmist has written: "Thy Word is a lamp unto my feet, and a light unto my path" (Psalm 119:105).

We also worship God through prayer. We talk with Him, we commune with Him, our mind touches His mind, and our spirit touches His Spirit. In our most humble state, we reach our highest self. George Meredith wrote: "He who rises from prayer a better man — his prayer is answered." One day a student entered Louis Pasteur's laboratory to find him bent over his microscope. "I thought you were praying," the student said. "I was," answered Pasteur and returned to his microscope. A little boy said, "Sometimes I pray; sometimes I just say my prayers."

Prayer is quietness, meditation, thanksgiving, communion, and worship. It is praise and a plea for others and for ourselves.

Through making a conscious effort to think about God, and creating in our being an awareness of Him through church attendance, the study of the Bible, and through prayer, we worship God. Yet, we worship Him in other very real ways, too:

> We chart our course
> We set our sails
> We tune our lives with God.

When we do our tasks about our home — willingly, lovingly, unselfishly — we worship God.

When we take the hand of a small child and show him our Master's world, we are worshiping God.

When we wash the grimy hands and faces of playful children, or put fresh sheets or warm blankets on a baby's bed, we are worshiping God.

When we brighten a lonely person's hours with a visit, a card, a flower, a walk, or a ride, we are worshiping God.

When we are kind to our neighbors and remember them in their needs, we are worshiping God.

When we help our church or community, however small we may feel that our task may be, we are worshiping God.

When we pat a little leaguer on the back, and watch him grow taller before our eyes, we are worshiping God.

When we attend a christening, visit a newborn, make a cake for a church supper, visit a hospital room, or write a note to help quell the sorrows of the grieved, we are worshiping God.

When we attend a funeral and are reminded that life extends beyond this moment, we are worshiping God.

In Dr. Walter Alvarez's column in the *News and Observer* on September 2, 1971, he quoted from a book by David Dunn, entitled, *Try Giving Yourself Away*: "More than anything else in the world, the world needs the healing influence of simple thoughtfulness, kindheartedness, and gratitude." Frank Crane wrote: "It takes so little to make people happy. Just a touch, if we know how to give it; just a word fitly spoken; just a readjustment of some bolt or pin or bearing in the delicate machinery of life."

Surely, if we love Him with all our heart, soul, and life, we cannot drift beyond Him, and *all* we do will glorify Him. We worship Him in moments of weakness in the helplessness of the words: "...My God, my God, why has thou forsaken me?" (Matthew 27:46). We worship Him in quiet faith in days of strength.

"To worship is," said the late William Temple:
"To quicken the conscience by the holiness of God,
To feel the mind with the truth of God,
To purge the imagination with the beauty of God,
To open the heart to the love of God, and
To devote the will to the purpose of God."

Most of all, we worship God through service to others. Did not Christ say, "A new commandment I give unto you, That ye love one another; as I have loved you, that ye also love one another" (John 13:34)? Did He not say, "...Inasmuch as ye have done it unto one of the least of these my brethren, ye have done it unto me" (Matthew 25:40)? Did He not say, "...Go ye into all the world,...." (Mark 16:15)?

What are the most meaningful words in the spiritual world: God, Jesus, Holy Spirit, love, forgiveness, others?

When Charles R. Brown of Yale University was addressing students on a western campus, he said, "I come from a larger university than this. It is larger than Columbia or Yale or all the universities combined. It is the University of life. Our colors are black and blue, for we learn our lesson by hard knocks. In this university there is but one examination day, and in that examination, there is but one question: 'What is life?' Let us ask the Great Teacher of all ages, and hear His answer by word and deed: Life is service! 'Even as the Son of man came not to be ministered unto, but to minister.' ." (Matthew 20:28).

Albert Schweitzer, in *Out of My Life and Thought*, tells of the time in his life when he determined to find something beyond himself to give his life to — and that was human service. William James said, "The great use of life is to spend it for something that outlasts it — others."

A missionary agricultural school in India closed its doors to all except Christian students. "A Christian graduate will teach others, and he is worth a hundred times as much as a non—Christian."

Adam Clarke, the great biblical scholar of 200 years ago, lies in Westminster Abbey. On his tomb is a candle, burned to the near socket, and around it these words: "In burning for others, he himself was consumed."

When the wife of the late Bishop Frederick Bohn Fisher took an Indian child into her arms, she did not know that the burning child was tortured by typhus, but three days later she was dead. Her heartbroken husband wrote this tribute for the stone that marks her resting place: "She died serving."

Father Damien, after working 11 years among the lepers at Molokai, was writing to a friend. He started to write the words, "the lepers"; suddenly he stopped as if paralyzed. He had seen the fatal white spot on his own hand. Then he crossed out the word *the* and wrote *we* lepers.

Communism says, "What is yours is mine, I'll take it." Capitalism says, "What's mine is my own, I'll keep it." Christianity says, "What's mine is ours, I'll share it."

Service to others gives Christianity a universal meaning. Someone has said that doctrine may divide, but service unites. Also, it has been said that service is the rent we pay for the space we occupy on God's earth. Too, service may be described as the material with which we build a stairway to God. How high is your stairway? How substantial is your stairway?

Service begins in a heart full of love which asks: How much do I really care? Do I love others enough to accept the challenges of learning to care for them and love them – not with my love, but with God's love so that I may know and practice forgiveness, humility, patience, understanding, and love?

Service should begin at home. Did you hear about the little girl who said, "Mommy, I wish you were as nice at home as you are in Sunday School"? Or about the little boy who asked his dad to describe a Christian. When the father finished, the child asked, "Dad, have I ever seen one?" Service begins at home and spreads to our neighbor and to the world.

How shall we serve? Let us serve humbly, forgetting self, lifting God and others – not caring who gets the credit – willing to do any task, great or small. May Jesus look at us and say as He did when He walked on earth: "She hath done what she could." Sometimes we become old or ill or weak, and we feel useless; but as long as we can pray for others, our lives are not lived in vain.

Let us serve quietly, even at times, secretly. We do

not serve to glorify self, but God. Sometimes I believe we do not get much credit in heaven for that which we get credit for on earth. We serve; God rewards!

Service is going, doing, and acting. It is also staying, waiting, hoping and praying.

An old Quaker of 82 years said, "I'm going to live 'til I die; then I'm going to live forever." This is the challenge of worship and service: to live, really live, until we die. We do not want to be like the little child who lost her birth certificate and cried, "I've lost my excuse for being born." Remember, "If my religion's not all that it ought to be, the trouble's not with God, the trouble's with me."

Thomas Carlyle wrote in *Sartor Resartus*: "Always there is a dark shadow in our sunshine — the shadow of ourselves." Are we big enough and Christian enough to forget self and serve others?

Longfellow wrote:

> "Let us then be up and doing
> With a heart for any fate;
> Still achieving, still pursuing
> Learn to labor and to wait."

Another writer, John Greenleaf Whittier, penned these words:

> "Our lives are albums written through
> With good or ill, with false or true;
> And as the blessed angels turn
> The pages of our years,
> God grant they read the good with smiles
> And blot the ill with tears."

Have you ever sung the following words by C.D. Meigs in the hymn, "Others"?

> "Lord, help me live from day to day
> In such a self-forgetful way
> That even when I kneel to pray
> My prayer shall be for others.
>
> "Others, Lord, yes, others,
> Let this my motto be,
> Help me to live for others,
> That I may live like Thee."

This is the secret: To be like Christ and to live for Christ, we must live for others.

John Greenleaf Whittier, in "Eternal Goodness," wrote:

> "I know not where His islands lift
> Their fronded palms in air;
> I only know I cannot drift
> Beyond his love and care."

We cannot drift beyond His love and care, for He has promised, "Lo, I am with you alway." Can we say that we are with Him — and that we will stay with Him always through worship in the beauty of holiness, and through serving Him with gladness and joy?

BLOOM WHERE YOU'RE TRANSPLANTED
(Not What We Have Lost)

In our day of jet transportation and computer communication, we are a nation and a people constantly "on the move." People are transferred or they change jobs almost overnight. Almost without notice, they are uprooted and transplanted. In the new environment, the challenge is always the same, "Bloom Where You're Planted."

The Bible is filled with people who were transplanted and who continued to serve God.

> "And the Lord said to Noah, come thou and all thy house unto the ark; for thee have I seen righteous before me in this generation" (Genesis 7:1).
>
> "Now the Lord said unto Abram (Abraham), Get thee out of thy country, and from thy kindred, and from thy father's house, unto a land that I will shew thee" (Genesis 12:1).
>
> "Then there passed by Midianites merchantmen; and they drew and lifted up Joseph out of the pit, and sold Joseph to the Ishmaelites

for twenty pieces of silver; and they brought Joseph into Egypt" (Genesis 37:28).

"Also, I heard the voice of the Lord, saying, Whom shall I send, and who will go for us? Then said I, Here am I; send me" (Isaiah 6:8).

"And a vision appeared to Paul in the night; There stood a man of Macedonia, and prayed him, saying, Come over into Macedonia, and help us" (Acts 16:9).

Also, sometimes we are transplanted by tragedy through personal illness, death of a loved one, or some fate of man or nature. What do we do then? How do we react? Maybe the answer is in "Not What We Have Lost."

What is life? How shall be explain our happiness, our success, our joy? Especially, how shall we understand our disappointments, our frustrations, our tears?

John Milton, for the last twenty years of his life, lived in a world of darkness; yet he gave light to the world through the brilliance of his mind and writings.

Ludwig Van Beethoven, after age twenty-eight, heard not a sound; yet he heard the music of the spheres through the inspiration of his mind.

John Bunyan sat locked in a dusty, dirty prison; yet he saw the struggle of all mankind and recorded it in *Pilgrim's Progress*, now translated into over one hundred languages.

Alfred Tennyson reached the "ripe" old age

of eighty-three; in his last years he wrote the immortal "Sunset and evening star, and one clear call for me..."

The Master heard the cries of the mob and felt the pain of death; yet He lifted His eyes to the greatest Hope of mankind.

But these were of the long ago. What about us today?

... A family watched its home as it was completely destroyed by fire; yet each could reach forth his hand and touch the living body of the others.

... A farmer walked across his hail-torn tobacco and corn fields; yet he could remember the part of the crop already harvested and the promise of another year.

... Another farmer saw his wheat fields leveled to the ground by a windstorm; yet he felt the burning sun drying the fallen wheat so that some of it could at least be saved and fed to the livestock on the farm.

... Still another tiller of the soil walked across his tornado-torn farm — buildings, home, crops — leveled to the ground; yet he realized that he himself still had the strength that had laid the foundations of each building, and planted the seed of the crops.

... A man awoke after several days of unconsciousness to find his body broken and torn — drained of all physical strength, perhaps forever; yet his mind was still his, uninjured and unscarred.

. . . A mother and father watched soldiers lift from a train a flag-draped coffin; yet the son and daughter beside them were reminders that though much was taken, much was left.

Could the answer to these be found in this thought from an unknown writer: "It is not what we have lost, but that which is left that we must consider." It is true that there are times when we must pause and shed a tear, even grieve perhaps. Our hearts bleed; our bodies ache. This is life! Yet, somewhere in the soul, that mysterious gift from God, we realize that through our faith and the use of time, God heals our minds as He heals our body when it is wounded or feverish or ill.

And so, like one of the followers of the Great Healer, we must try to "forget those things that are behind and press on. . ." We must pick up the broken pieces, and leave, except for an occasional memory, that which is lost and build on that which is left.